The Ozark Mountains

ARKANSAS
Her Beauty & Character

Text by
J.J. THOMPSON

Photographs by
KAY DANIELSON

Design by
SUZANNE KITTRELL

August House / Little Rock
PUBLISHERS

Printed in the United States of America

10 9 8 7 6 5 4 3 2 1

LIBRARY OF CONGRESS CATALOGING-IN-PUBLICATION DATA

Thompson, J. J., 1962-
Arkansas, her beauty and character / text by J.J. Thompson ;
photographs by Kay Danielson ; design by Suzanne Kittrell.
p.   cm.
Includes index.
ISBN 0-87483-092-3 (alk. paper) : $34.95
1. Arkansas—Description and travel—1981-
2. Arkansas—Civilization.
3. Arkansas—Description and travel—1981—Views.
I. Title.
F415.T46   1989
976.7053—dc19   89-30320
                                                     CIP

First Edition, 1989

Typography by Lettergraphics, Memphis, Tennessee
Project direction by Ted Parkhurst

All photographs in this book are by Kay Danielson except for
those otherwise cited in the caption.

This book is printed on archival-quality paper which meets the
guidelines for performance and durability of the Committee on
Production Guidelines for Book Longevity of the Council on
Library Resources.

AUGUST HOUSE, INC.   PUBLISHERS   LITTLE ROCK

For Joe,
for making me laugh
even when I didn't feel like it.
JJT

To Arkansas,
certainly a land of opportunity.
KD

CONTENTS

AN ARKANSAS ALBUM

The Buffalo River

Buffalo Point

View from Wilhelmina Lodge

Calico Rock

Cabot

Photographs on these pages were taken in the locations referenced on map.

Near the Cossatot

Bear Creek

Crystal Lake

Leaves stir as fall nears an end.

*Waterfalls are plentiful in the rivers and
streams of Arkansas's mountains.*

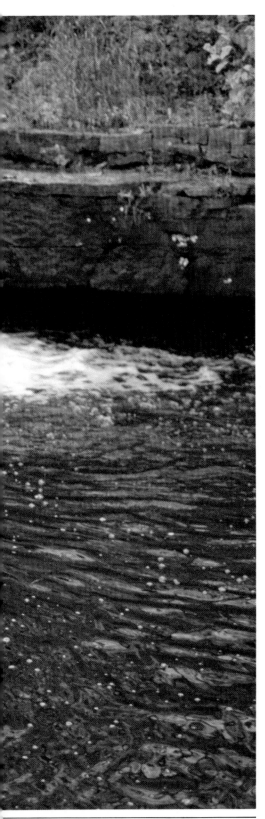

PLACE

Isn't it amazing how Arkansans are often the last to realize what a great place they get to call home?

We who live here tend to take for granted all the riches Arkansas has to offer. Her unique heritage. Her relatively unspoiled natural beauty. Her great opportunities for work and play. Her promises for an exciting future.

Yet many of our people wander away, hoping to find good fortune and great fame. Others move here expecting to stay no longer than necessary. But many who leave soon return, and those who plan to depart often find they never do. Something about the friendly faces, the fresh air, the peaceful countryside, the bustling towns, and the quality of life these together offer, form a bond that's not easily broken.

Grain elevators, such as these near Brinkley, are a common sight in the ricelands of Arkansas.

Actors rehearse for one of the first performances in the new Arkansas Repertory Theatre in Little Rock.

Not even a musician stirs on stage during the early morning hours after an old-time music festival in Mountain View the previous night.

The wonders of Arkansas are many—and, indeed, one of its nicknames is the Wonder State. Where else can one find rugged mountain trails only scant miles away from rich delta flatland? Big-city culture hand in hand with down-home hospitality? Wineries and catfish farms separated only by a few counties? Record-breaking watermelons grown in the same town that produces some of the world's finest stereo speakers? Only in Arkansas.

No doubt the state is richer because of her complexities, so they should be explained, examined, and appreciated again and again. For it's this variety, and the way people here have learned to live and grow with it, that make Arkansas the unique place it is.

When you think about it, Arkansas is a lot like an afghan, one that's been made with yarns of every color and tied together with all the knots in a knitter's repertoire. The different hues and weights of the yarns, the unique combination of knots, and the varying texture that results—that's Arkansas.

But analogies don't really get at the nature of this place. One has to wonder if that can be done, whether all the wonderful diversity and complexities found here can fit into a single perspective. The only way possible is to take a look at the land and its riches and at the people and the kind of lives they lead.

Photographs on these pages were taken in the locations referenced on map.

1. *Near Mountain View, pp. 18-19*
2. *Brinkley, p. 19*
3. *Little Rock, p. 20*
4. *Mountain View, p. 21*
5. *Little Rock, pp. 22-23*

The lights of Little Rock sparkle across the
Arkansas River.

*Winding highways provide some of the best
views of foliage in the state.*

Maybe the best way to start this exploration is by taking to the roads of Arkansas, a geography lesson in their own right. In the east they are flat and straight, cutting through wide, open expanses of fields and farmlands. Highways in western Arkansas, though, seem contorted by comparison as they twist, turn, climb, and descend mountain after mountain. And no calendar is needed to indicate the seasons when you have the trees on the roadsides to clue you in. Often they are so numerous and stand so close together they form an opaque curtain down each side of the road—emerald in the spring and summer, multicolored in the fall, and a lacy sheath of intertwining limbs during the winter.

The setting sun casts long shadows as the moon rises at the end of a fall day.

Nature displays her colors throughout the state in the most surprising places, such as this ground apricot on a mountain trail.

Speaking of seasons, little in life approaches the beauty of an Arkansas spring, which steps gingerly into the state during the early weeks of March or sometimes as early as February. By the first of April, the season has completed its sweep through the region, leaving in its trail a state literally blooming with color—the vibrant yellow of daffodils, the fresh white and pink of dogwood blossoms, and the intense lavender of redbud trees. The gifts of spring brighten lawns, fields, and forests alike, replaced week after week by the equally brilliant flowers of summer,

lasting all through the long warm months. Yet not even the spring can offer a thrill equal to that of waking on one of those rare winter mornings when the night has spread a blanket of snow, leaving all of outdoors white and gleaming. And what can compare to the fresh, clean fragrance that lingers in the air after a shower on a hot summer afternoon?

An artist painting the overall beauty of Arkansas would find it quite easy. She probably would begin by drawing a squiggly line down the right side of the canvas. That would be the Missis-

sippi River, which forms Arkansas's eastern border. Another blue line—this one the Arkansas River—would be drawn diagonally, cutting the state into northeastern and southwestern halves. The entire area of the state would be filled in with varying tones of greens and browns. Broad easy strokes would depict the rich land of the eastern delta with its cotton and soybeans as well as the state's central plains of rice fields, while much more rugged strokes would suggest dense forests in the south and mountains in the north and west.

The scenic Buffalo River provides a spectacular view.

Hot water gurgles from the earth in one of the popular "good luck" springs at the Hot Springs National Park.

Photographs on these pages were taken in the locations referenced on map.

1. *Route 23 North, pp. 24-25*
2. *Buffalo River, p. 27.*
3. *Hot Springs National Park, p. 28*
4. *Calico Rock, p. 29*

More than sixty percent of Arkansas is forest land that, pretty as it is, provides the resources for such practical items as lumber, paper, and cardboard. The abundant lakes, rivers, and streams not only ensure that Arkansas's citizens have water—a commodity becoming more precious every day—but also give her residents and visitors countless hours of recreation. It's no wonder that fishing, waterskiing, motorboating, sailing, canoeing, and kayaking are all favorite pastimes in Arkansas.

This fishing dock on the White River near Calico Rock is a popular place for fishermen.

Yet the varied topography is only one of the delights of the land. Beneath the soil are found all kinds of treasures—from oil in the south around El Dorado to diamonds at Murfrees-boro to the thermal waters of Hot Springs. And Arkansas leads the nation in the production of bauxite, as well as processing stores of natural gas, bro-mine, silica stone, ceramic clay, chalk, gypsum, and other valuable minerals.

Dancers celebrate Christmas the old-fashioned way at the Old State House.

Yet, as wondrous a place as Arkansas is naturally, one can't really capture the character of the state without telling about its richest resource—its people.

First of all, a few generalities. Of the 2.3 million people who live here, 39 percent live in cities while the rest live on farms or in small towns. Nearly 400,000 are black and 20,000 Hispanic. Most Arkansans still mark their ballots for the Democratic candidates, at least locally, and most still put on their best and head for the sanctuary each Sunday morning. Some of the wealthiest of the nation's wealthy live here—Sam Walton, J.B. Hunt, and Witt and Jack Stephens, for instance—and the state has her share of the nation's homeless as well. But most people are somewhere in between, some just getting by, many others making their way quite comfortably.

A child takes part in a re-enactment gathering, an activity designed to keep Arkansas's heritage alive.

A better way to capture the essence of Arkansas, though, is to tell about specific people—those men and women who work and play and dream day after day. They, after all, are the ones who make a difference, who make up the collective character of this state.

Meet Ruth Ann Wise, the guide at Toltec Mounds State Park who makes the children in her tour groups feel as important as the grownups. Or Lucy Babcock, the Little Rock poetry editor who used her cane to beat an attacker when a young woman screamed for help. Or Hayward McManus, a retired gentleman in Newport who offered to guide a visitor through the Jacksonport Courthouse Museum, telling all the interesting tidbits and stories he knew about the place.

Experiences, some of them unique to Arkansas, also enhance the definition of this place. They can show how people here truly care for each other, be they good friends, mere acquaintances, or absolute strangers. For example, when a family member is ill or has died, you can count on neighbors and friends to bring casseroles, breads, and cookies. And when towns face severe losses from such tragedies as tornadoes or fires, people from all around the state are quick to send food, clothing, and money. These kinds of deeds occur day after day in Arkansas. The excitement of a University of Arkansas Razorback football game, on the other hand, is a happier experience that also binds the state together: the sea of red and white in the stands matches the colors of the players' uniforms, and cheers and music can be heard for miles around.

The Courthouse Square fills with people each year during the Pink Tomato Festival in Warren.

The Old Soldier's Parade marches through
Heber Springs in front of the downtown
Cleburne County Courthouse.

Photographs on these
pages were taken in the
locations referenced on
map.

1. *Little Rock,* p. 30
2. *Warren,* p. 32
3. *Heber Springs,* p. 33
4. *Stuttgart,* p. 33

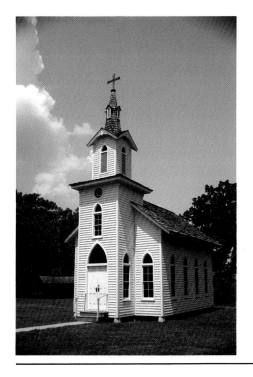

*An old church building on the grounds of
the Agricultural Museum at Stuttgart has
seen many a service and celebration in years
gone by.*

Historic buildings, such as this log cabin in
Prairie Grove Battlefield State Park, still
dot Arkansas's landscape.

Yet another look at the many aspects of Arkansas is through the kaleidoscope of communities and towns where the state's poeple—some of them here all their lives, some who've decided to settle here, and others who have moved back "home"—have planted their deep and loyal roots. Arkansas has a pleasant blend of rural lifestyles on the farm, slow-paced living in small towns, urban experiences in larger cities, the energies of youth in college towns, and the quieter contentment of people who have settled in retirement villages.

Dotted all along the back roads of Arkansas are communities that are small in land area and population but big in pride. Of the people who live there—in Higden and Hermitage, Taylor and Tollette—most know each other, look out for each other, and, of course, care about each other. With often no more than a general store, a post office, and a gas station in the area, they've learned the importance of "making do" and of helping out a neighbor.

At the Forrest City Harvest Festival you can buy just about anything, even your very own scarecrow.

There's nothing better than companionship and a warm spring day.

The historic golden dome, which can be seen for miles, is a familiar sight in Pine Bluff.

Many small towns like Magnolia, Berryville, Conway, and Helena, with Victorian-style homes next door to newer brick ones, still center around the town square. There the courthouse stands proudly, and a Methodist, Baptist, and Presbyterian church, post office, and library usually aren't too far away. While Friday nights find the majority of the townspeople rooting for the local high school team, weekdays see them busily working at local banks, shops, and businesses. Politics and local school matters concern everyone in these towns, not just a select few. Arkansas also has its share of tourist resorts, Hot Springs and Eureka Springs being two of the favorites. Both cling to hillsides and possess distinctive charms. Hot Springs has drawn people for years to its steamy, invigorating baths, its colorful thoroughbred racetrack, and more recently to a theme park, museum, and other family attractions. Eureka Springs, an artists' haven, is a Victorian world with bed-and-breakfast inns in gabled houses and a trolley that travels its hilly, winding streets. The Great Passion Play is itself an Arkansas institution, as is Onyx Cave Park with its formations of stalactites and stalagmites.

Corner grocery stores play an important role in small communities.

Sometimes the love of a pet is all that's needed.

A shopping center in west Little Rock dons holiday finery.

Bridges span the Arkansas River.

The historic Villa Marre in Little Rock holds a treasured place in the hearts of many Arkansans.

And then there are the state's larger cities, where people live and work in urban settings much like those in any other part of the country. The greater Little Rock area, the largest, tops a population figure of 535,000, and its neighborhoods and subdivisions have spread for miles in all directions. Even so, a typical story is that of the couple who chose to move their family to Arkansas's capital because they were thrilled with the attractive first impression it made on them. As they flew over Little Rock and North Little Rock for the first time, they admired the way the sister cities flank the clean, broad Arkansas River. Driving into downtown they were happy to see the cities' attractive skylines, not cluttered and not lost in smog. They appreciated the cultural advantages of the place— ballet, theater, symphonies—and liked the fact that hunting, fishing, and hiking are only a few minutes' drive from the center of town.

A lone fisherman takes advantage of the last light of the day.

Giant cypress trees can be found growing in the swampy waters of the Delta.

Of course the Little Rock–North Little Rock area is not the only metropolitan area in the state. Fort Smith, Pine Bluff, and the Fayetteville-Springdale-Rogers area also fit into this category, as do large towns or small cities like Jonesboro, West Memphis, El Dorado, and Hot Springs. The diversity of the city dwellers' backgrounds and interests produce a vitality that can only be described as urban. And the fast pace so closely associated with city life is a natural product of the many work-related, charitable, and recreational activities in full swing there.

Taken individually, each aspect of the state—the natural wonders, the people, and the cities—tells a separate, revealing, and meaningful tale about a life that is at once peaceful and bustling, traditional and progressive, agricultural and industrial. Taken together, they tell about a single place—a place called Arkansas.

Photographs on these pages were taken in the locations referenced on map.

Bright colors, both natural and man-made, line the streets of Shirley.

DATES TO REMEMBER

10,000 B.C.	Paleo-Indian culture
8,000	Archaic period
500	Woodland culture
700 A.D.	Mississippian culture
1541	Hernando De Soto crossed the great river and explored Arkansas
1673	Marquette and Joliet explored the Mississippi River bordering Arkansas
1682	La Salle claimed the Mississippi River basin, of which present-day Arkansas was part, for France, and named it Louisiana
1686	De Tonti established Arkansas Post, the first permanent settlement in Arkansas
1763	France ceded Louisiana to Spain
1800	Spain ceded Louisiana to France
1803	United States purchased Louisiana from France
1806	District of Arkansas created
1819	Arkansas Territory organized
1821	Capital moved to Little Rock from Arkansas Post

1836	Arkansas admitted as twenty-fifth state to the Union
1846–48	Arkansas participated in the Mexican War
1853	Arkansas's first railroad company organized
1861	Arkansas seceded from Union and joined Confederacy
1862	Civil War battles fought at Pea Ridge and Prairie Grove
1863	Arkansas's Confederate capital moved to Washington; Union army occupied Little Rock
1865	Arkansas's Confederate government surrendered
1871	State university established at Fayetteville
1874	End of post–Civil War Reconstruction in Arkansas
1879	First telephones installed in Arkansas
1888	First electric lights installed in Arkansas
1906	Diamonds discovered in Pike County
1917–18	Arkansans served in First World War
1920	Oil discovered in Ouachita and Union Counties
1928	Senator Joe T. Robinson became Democratic vice-presidential candidate
1932	Hattie Caraway of Arkansas elected first female U.S. Senator nationwide
1941–45	Arkansans served in Second World War
1955	Arkansas Industrial Development Commission established
1957	Little Rock school desegregation crisis
1970	McClellan-Kerr Arkansas River Navigation Project completed
1986	Arkansas celebrated sesquicentennial of statehood

Arkansans enjoy watching the increasing beauty of the southern magnolia blossom as it slowly opens its petals.

*The folk arts are a substantial business in
Arkansas.*

WORK

The next time you hear someone mention the "land of opportunity" and don't know what he's talking about, be sure to ask. Chances are, he'll reply without hesitation. Even a safer bet, he'll say proudly, "Arkansas."

The phrase "land of opportunity" is full of meaning for a lot of people. Many men and women have settled and toiled within Arkansas's boundaries with aspirations of succeeding financially and making a name for themselves. Happily for them and for those who live here, a good many of them have done so.

To Arkansans, some names of those families who went to work years ago are so familiar they have become household words, names like Coleman Dairy, Tipton Hurst Florists, Franke's

Systematics, Inc., develops computer programs and software for banking concerns across the nation. (Courtesy of Systematics, Inc.)

Cafeterias, and Wiederkehr Wines. And there are quite a few that have become just as well known beyond Arkansas's borders—Dillard's Department Stores, Tyson Chicken, and Stephens, Inc., to list just a few. Others, maybe not so widely known, have for years held honored and respected positions within their own communities. Take Stinson Jewelers in Camden, for instance, or Couch's Corner Barbecue in Jonesboro. To the founders of all these businesses, Arkansas indeed has been a "land of opportunity."

Yet that little catch-phrase, one the state has used as her official nickname, only hints at the business and entrepreneurial success stories that are part of the fabric of Arkansas. Again the true heroes of these stories are the people of the state. Today's work spirit, after all, was clearly foreshadowed in the histories of our state's founders. Those individuals faced without fear the tremendous task of transforming wilderness into a livable, civilized state. They knew well the value of doing one's best, no matter what obstacles or challenges loomed ahead. The pride and perseverance involved in making that transformation have been passed from mother and father to son and daughter, generation after generation.

In short, those ideals planted in the fertile soil of our citizenry by the early pioneers—dedication, flexibility, a willingness to take risks, ingenuity, pride in one's work, and the desire to improve and grow—are the same qualities that make business endeavors flourish today. To find them, one has only to take a look around, and not a very long or hard one at that.

Many Arkansans are engaged in agriculture, which accounts for the state's production of a wide variety of crops.

Period cabins like this one are on display at the Ozark Folk Center in Mountain View.

Just south of Pine Bluff is a little town called Grady sitting like a small island of old wooden buildings in a sea of green farmland. Not many people live here; the sign at either side of town lists a population figure only three digits long. There's a white, wood-frame store with a big front porch in the heart of town, and several houses with tidy fenced-in yards and pickup trucks parked in the driveways. A short distance from town, just off Highway 11, stands a colorful sign pointing to Carpenter's Produce Farm.

Despite the fact that the Carpenters are a good-sized group of sisters, brothers, sons, daughters, nephews, nieces, and cousins, the family's three houses at the end of the long dirt drive are empty at midday. "You'll find 'em out past the green beans," a neighbor tells a couple of city folks who don't know a green bean plant from a common weed. But, yes, there they are, a colorful group wearing cool, cotton print shirts and dresses, jeans, and overalls, and hats or bandannas to protect their heads from the scalding June sun. They explain that they are working the fields of collard greens. This expanse of green is surrounded by other green seas, some of which are dotted with bright yellows, red, and deep purples, like fish hiding in the waves. Those are summer squash, zucchini, okra, tomatoes, blueberries, sweet potatoes, purple-hulled peas, and bell peppers.

Abraham Carpenter, Jr., a young man, enjoys his work but at the same time is serious about his role as family businessman and, with his father, farm manager. While he talks about the family enterprise, his watchful eyes never leave the others, busily picking greens, and at one point he pauses in mid-sentence and calmly urges a brother, "Tell those two (picking greens) to quit standing up so much."

Abraham graduated from Grady High School in 1980 near the top of his class. At that time, especially with several academic scholarships offered to

Abraham Carpenter, Jr., sells his produce twice a week at the Downtown Farmers' Market in Little Rock.

Arkansas is well known for its production of cotton, peaches, and rice.

him, he knew he was about to make a decision that would shape the rest of his life. "I knew to get enough schooling to get a good-paying job would mean at least four and probably six or more years," he says in his quiet, even voice. By that time, adding to his options, his father had purchased land and started a vegetable produce farm. During his high school years, Abraham witnessed the farm's quick spurt from just five acres to many times that. "I decided to come out here and put all I had into the vegetables," he says as his nephew drives by on a tractor, leaving a trail of flying, then floating, dust. And most of his siblings have followed suit.

Between Abraham Jr. and his seven brothers and sisters—James, Ruby, Betty Clark and Bobby Clark (they married brothers, who now also work on the farm), Danny, Albert, and Terry—and their children, the Carpenter clan numbers almost thirty. With such a hearty crew, they've been able to plant

350 acres of various crops. While most of the family works in the fields, Abraham explains, one of his sisters babysits, his mother cooks the meals (which, of course, include plenty of fresh vegetables), and he's out on the road many days making deliveries to distribution centers of grocery store chains they supply as well as negotiating new business deals.

"If you're a vegetable producer, you don't get much rest," Abraham notes—not complaining, mind you, but simply stating a fact. And he means what he says. During the long growing season between mid-spring and mid-autumn when they are not only working the farm but also loading up refrigerated trucks and heading to the farmers' markets in Little Rock and Pine Bluff, the family members are rolling out of bed by 2:00 a.m. And even on off days, when they do get to sleep "late," they still beat the sun up by a couple of hours. "We work sixteen to twenty hours a day most days, except on Sundays, when we work a half-day unless we're really busy," says Carpenter. "There's a lot of dedication here," he muses, adding, "It takes that, too. I don't think you can make it without it. . . . Our family was very close growing up. We have a good mother and a good father and they've taught us to stick together and work together—then you can accomplish anything you want."

Bales of cotton in Lonoke await shipment to textile mills.

Catfish are taken from the pond to be processed at the Harrison family farm near Carlisle. Arkansas is the one of the country's leading producers of commercial catfish.

Don't ask the Harrisons of Carlisle to go fishing—not if you mean just sitting on the bank with a cane pole in hand. "If you can't get ten thousand pounds a lick, we don't want to go fishing. Talk about boring," Debbye Harrison says, only half joking, while watching her husband, Carter, and sons, Chris and Bryce, haul in a net-load of catfish. They are seining, a process that at the Harrisons' farm means dragging a huge net across the bottom of one of their catfish ponds. They wade chest-high into the water with the full net in order to sort the just-the-right-size fish—two to four pounds—from the not-big-enough-yet ones, tossing out a turtle or two and keeping an eye out for snakes. It's just part of the normal catfish farming routine. And catfish farming is only one part of the Harrisons' multifaceted business.

Humor and work go hand in hand at the City Bakery in Hope. The sign on the door says, "Eat Here, We Knead the Dough."

Photographs on these pages were taken in the locations referenced on map.

Historic War Eagle Mill draws tourists year-round and is well-known for its annual arts and crafts fair.

In addition to raising the fish from fingerling size to maturity—a three-year chore in itself—the Harrisons process it and sell it to individuals, grocery stores, and a few restaurants as well as supplying their own catering business, King Kat. "I see the catering business slowly overtaking the farm and processing business," Debbye says in the large kitchen of the family's brick home. If you glance out the front window, you can see the King Kat Caterers sign by the front drive that welcomes customers and visitors alike.

When they first started out in the mid-1960s as a young couple in business with Debbye's parents, fish farming wasn't even considered a career option, nor was catering. "We had this piece of land that wouldn't [even] grow sage-grass very well, so we had a quail shooting preserve." But when the quail all died of cholera, the Harrisons took the first in a series of new career paths and decided to dam up a natural reserve on the property and raise fish. That one small pond has grown to thirty-five acres of ponds, and, Debbye says, theirs is one of the smallest catfish farms in Arkansas—a state that is one of the leading catfish producers in the nation.

"Fish farming as an occupation is probably forty years old," explains Debbye, a history buff who teaches social studies at a nearby high school. "Carter and Daddy just kind of eased into it" in the late '60s, making them the first catfish farmers in central Arkansas, and then Carter and Debbye went into business for themselves in 1977. When they began, the Harrisons processed and sold only the fish they had raised, but soon the demand for their fish was

*The museum at Arkansas City houses
artifacts of Arkansas's past.*

more than their ponds could support. So they increased their processing capabilities and started buying fish from neighboring farmers to process and sell. That way they could know the source of their fish, making sure they were healthy, of good quality, and most importantly, tasty.

Then came the day a man asked them to cater a catfish dinner for a social gathering, the first time they would do such a thing. Soon they received another such request and then another. "Daddy and Carter did the first couple of meals together and Mother and I made the slaw," Debbye remembers. Their equipment con-

sisted of borrowed cookers, a pair of tongs, and pasteboard beer boxes and paper towels for serving the fish. Now they have two fully equipped trailers custom-designed by Carter, complete with stainless steel walls, commercial fryers, hot and cold water, and all the other extras that guarantee quality.

"We used to have a rule that we wouldn't cater more than four times a week," Harrison says, dishing up a plate of the crispy fried fish, a typical once-or-more-a-week meal for the family. "Now we have a rule that we won't do more than four a day." And that's been without advertising much. Carter Harrison, dipping a bite of fish into

The lumber industry plays an important role in Arkansas's economy.

tartar sauce, explains, "Most of it has been word of mouth. Somebody eats at one meal and suggests us for another." They've catered everything from private parties to public festivals, even taking the whole setup to Washington, D.C., to serve the U.S. Senate several times.

So far, being flexible and open to new avenues for their business has proved to be the right approach for the Harrisons. They probably haven't made their last change, either. Not too long ago a man called, almost angry. He had tasted some of their fish and fixings at an outdoor festival and had searched all the state's phone books since then

for their restaurant. "We don't have one," Debbye told him, adding that they'd be serving at another festival in a few days. He was pacified, but he didn't know that he had hit on a project idea the family had been toying with. "That will probably be the next phase of the business," Debbye says.

Except for a couple of phone calls, it's pretty quiet—almost peaceful—on an overcast Saturday morning in the offices and pressroom of the *Cabot Star-Herald.* "Nobody realizes we're here" this early on a weekend morning, Cone Magie, the editor and publisher of the small-town weekly newspaper, says to explain the near-silence. If they did, he implies, they'd be in, buying ads, submitting wedding announcements, or simply letting their opinions about local issues be known. That participation, which amounts to almost a feeling of community ownership, is the joy and sometimes the headache of running a small-town paper. Dressed casually in an open-collar shirt, talking about his recent travels to foreign lands, national politics, and concerns facing newspapers near the end of the twentieth century, Cone seems to be happy—content, you might say, with his life and career. But he and his wife, Betty, a respected newspaperwoman and former president of the Arkansas Press Association and the Arkansas Press Women's Association, worked long and hard to reach this pinnacle. And the prospects for success weren't always certain.

"When we started," Betty remembers, "we started with a three-by-five file cabinet, a portable typewriter, and an old Sears dinette table that we ordered when we were going to the University [of Arkansas] and the chair to it that I had rewoven the bottom of." Those pieces, plus a cot for their three-year-old, made up the meager furnishings of their first office.

That was back in 1955, soon after Betty's brother had proposed that they

come to Lonoke County from Washington, D.C., where Cone was working. Her brother told them that there were some people in Cabot wanting a hometown paper. Would Cone and Betty be interested in taking on the project? Indeed they were. Cone had been out of the newspaper field for several years by then, but he had never lost his love for the business. After all, he had seen it from all angles. He and his brother delivered the *Arkansas Gazette* as youngsters in England, the small Lonoke County town where Cone grew up and eventually edited the high school newspaper. "I think that's where it got in my blood. You know that they say newspaper, the ink, gets in your blood," Cone says reflectively, sipping black coffee at his desk.

He continues the story. After fighting for three years in World War II in the South Pacific, he came home and asked Betty, his "girl" from schooldays, to marry him. And, Betty adds, she didn't just get a husband out of the marriage, but a lifetime career in journalism as well. After Cone earned a degree from the University of Arkansas, a couple of stints with newspapers in northwest Arkansas were followed by editing jobs with the Farm Bureau in Little Rock, Iowa, and then Washington.

When Betty's brother called, it didn't take much deliberation to decide to head back home and follow through with their dream; the Magies just didn't realize what a risk they were taking. Not only were their office furnishings sparse, Betty says, but "what we didn't know was that the town was too small for a hometown, homeprinted paper." Sometimes a lack of knowledge is a

The Ozark Mountains remain one of the state's most distinctive—and spellbinding—features.

good thing, and that certainly was the case then. Starting with almost nothing, the Magies involved a students' club at Cabot High School in selling subscriptions. By the time they sent out the first issue of the *Cabot Star* a few weeks later, they were delivering to four hundred homes and businesses.

The next decades included more risks and more growth. The purchase of the *Cabot Herald,* which had previously been written and printed in Lonoke; the addition of two other county papers—the *Lonoke Democrat* and the *Carlisle Independent;* the change to an offset press; and bigger buildings in Cabot and Lonoke are concrete indications of the effort they've put in over the years. "It's been hard work, but it's been rewarding work," Betty says. And the Magies do work. They write, edit, lay out pages, sell advertising, do a lot of their own janitorial chores, and on some mornings can even be seen out delivering papers. After all, Cone says, "You can write your heart out, but if that thing doesn't get delivered, it doesn't do you a bit of good."

With the circulation of the three papers now totaling more than nine thousand a week, the Magies know they have paved the way for their children, two of whom are working with them and learning the business, and fulfilled the desires of an area with a lot of hometown pride. "I think our goal has been to build our community and make it a better place," Cone says. His wife agrees. "We feel that if we do our job well that it will help to build our area. And that's what we've tried to do."

To think it all started when they were willing to take the risk to come home to Cabot with only a small file cabinet and a portable typewriter.

Rice goes from field to storage in the flat-lands of Arkansas, the country's leading producer of rice.

A few years ago Bill Valentine, longtime general manager of the Arkansas Travelers baseball team, called a salesman about getting some hand lotion and dispensers for the women's restrooms at Ray Winder Field, home of the team. The salesman, taken by surprise, replied earnestly that hand lotion didn't belong in a ball park. "You're supposed to be selling me," Bill says he remembers telling him, and adds proudly, "Now the ladies come, they say they can't believe it, they've got hand lotion in there. Well, that's a promotion, it's a little extra, it's something nice."

A little unconventional, maybe, but no matter. That's Bill's style and a good example of the way he's run Ray Winder Field since he took over in 1976. The fast-moving, fast-talking man, who as a boy worked at the very same ball park as a baseball shagger, points out of his office door to the parking lots where, in an earlier time, trolley cars would line up and wait for the fans to come pouring out of the gates at the end of a game. But the change from trolleys to automobiles isn't the only one Bill has witnessed over the years. Now that the Travelers are a farm team of the St. Louis Cardinals and not their own local entity, fan loyalty is not what it used to be. So he's come up with myriad ingenious ways to keep the park a fun, popular place to be.

For example, there are very few nights of the season when a fan can't find some way to get into the park free. That's because Bill has found sponsors to buy the park out. One night will be Pepsi Night, another Arctic Ice Night, and still another Law School Night. And soon he realized that only one was not enough. "You've got to embellish on it. . . . So I started double, triple, quadruple promoting," he says. But perhaps the most clever attraction he's come up with is his unique giveaway promotion. That came about when "I was reading a magazine and they were giving away Virginia Slims datebooks, sort of nice hardbacks," Bill explains between answering a busy phone that has him talking to local sportscasters and fans asking about upcoming games. But, he says, never missing a word of the conversation despite the constant interruptions, he realized that any time a company had a promotion they had to overstock what they were giving away. "So I thought, 'Well, every

company does that, so what do they do with what's left?' Most of the time it goes in the garbage, that's what," Bill proclaims in a pace that could rival the speed of any fastball.

"So I wrote to the cigarette companies and to Kodak and to Aunt Jemima Foods and Campbell Soups" and offered them a bargain. He proposed that if they would send him all their leftovers after a promotion ended, he would give them out at the door (if there were eighty-two Sanka mugs left over, he'd declare Sanka Night at the ball park—free mugs to the first eighty-two through the gate) and everyone would profit. "We're still getting it into

the hands of the public," he wrote them. "You're gaining because you're not throwing these in some dump. You've probably got $1, $1.50, $2 invested in each one, so you're getting the value; I'm getting the value because the people who are coming to the ball park are getting a free gift."

Now companies call him all the time.

What's more, his ingenious schemes have worked wonders. Since 1980 annual attendance at the ballpark has been over 200,000—the highest ever, Bill says. And, even more importantly, the fans not only enjoy good baseball, they enjoy Ray Winder Field.

Bill Valentine takes advantage of one of the perks of his job as general manager of Arkansas Travelers baseball team at Ray Winder Field in Little Rock.

Yarnell's Ice Cream Company at Searcy, a leading producer of ice cream and dairy treats in this region of the country, has come a long way since its early days when ice cream was cranked by hand.

A few years ago A. Rogers Yarnell, the third-generation president of family-owned Yarnell's Ice Cream Company in Searcy, had to determine the future of the business. To grow as he had planned, should the company stay in Searcy or had the time come to move elsewhere? After much deliberation, the final decision was to stay in Searcy. It wasn't just financial considerations or the dreaded hassles of moving that kept Yarnell's in familiar territory. "Probably the most important factor is the quality of the people that we've been able to attract in this area," Rogers says, leaning back comfortably in his office chair, tapping his pen in a slow, even beat on his desk. And that concern for a top-quality worker most certainly extends

to concern for an equally top-of-the-line product.

Even when his grandfather bought a small, bankrupt ice cream company back in the early years of the Depression, the commitment to quality was there. Rogers remembers the family stories of those days well. "My grandfather used to go to Bald Knob, Arkansas, when it was the strawberry capital of the world, and he would pick the very best berries, bring them back, and our team members here would cap them by hand and we would sugar them and they'd be used in our ice cream."

That tradition of using only the best is one to which Rogers adheres. While the wooden ice cream freezers of old have been replaced by state-of-the-art

Parking meters found all over the world probably were made in Arkansas, either at POM, Inc., in Russellville or Duncan Industries in Harrison.

Arkansas leads the world in production of commercial broiler chickens, and research is continually being done to create new and better strains.

stainless steel vats and high-speed freezers, the quality of the ingredients has remained high. And many of those ingredients are bought right here in the state, he adds. "As far as the milk and the cream, which are the two most important ingredients in making good ice cream, that's virtually all acquired within the state of Arkansas. Certain ingredients are not available in Arkansas—Arkansas doesn't grow pistachio nuts. If a quality product is available locally, we'll acquire it here. If it's not, we go to where we can find the best products."

The tradition has certainly played a part in the company's success. Yarnell's has almost a cult following of people who love their ice cream, and that alone keeps the Arkansas-based company far out of the shadow of larger ice cream companies in the nation. "We must create an image and be able to fulfill that image in the minds of our consumers against companies that don't always have to make a profit in that particular year or that particular quarter." Rogers says that the popularity of Yarnell's products, along with the success they've experienced, makes expansion a viable step. The construction noises coming from other areas in the plant are a constant reminder that that indeed is happening.

Even with the recent emphasis on growth, quality remains the highest

A huge hub of railroad activity lies in North Little Rock.

priority at Yarnell's. In fact, Rogers says, all "team members"—as Yarnell's employees are considered—share the responsibility for ensuring that every carton of ice cream produced is the very best possible. The actual testing of the product is done very methodically. A group consisting of the manufacturing manager, the quality assurance lab technician, and the production line manager take the first, a middle, and the last carton off each production run and slice them down the center. All three team members taste samples from each carton and rank the delicacy for four subjective means of evaluation and then for a number of objective means determined in the lab. "Those three people," Rogers explains, "determine whether or not that product is satisfactory or unsatisfactory for release to the public. That's done on every production run."

That's quality assurance.

Commercial wine and grape products have been staple products in the Altus area for more than a century.

A century or so ago, no one had heard of a BB gun. Now, however, anyone who has heard of a BB gun has heard of Daisy, probably the best-known airgun rifle seller in the nation. And that status is hard to ignore when you're standing in the middle of the museum at Daisy Manufacturing, Inc., in Rogers. The museum, full of guns representing about every model Daisy has produced in the last hundred years or more, is across the lobby from the main plant, where every day three to five thousand toy guns and airguns are assembled and shipped to stores across the world.

David Lewis, who has worked at Daisy for several years, still seems impressed with the quality of work the company does as he leads a tour of the plant—three thousand feet of machines stamping, cutting, and pressing bits of metal; and people pressing the right levers, testing guns as they come off the assembly line, and taking care of all the intricate details that go into the making and packaging of a Daisy rifle.

With close to 650 employees, Daisy is one of the state's largest companies, David explains as he picks up and examines a tiny chunk of wire about to be processed into a round BB shot. Though new jobs are being created regularly, making new faces common on the factory floor as well as upstairs in the executive offices, "there's not a lot of turnover here," David says. "We've got a lot of people who've been working here, especially in the plant, for over thirty years. . . . In the office, you've got a lot of what might be called lifers— a lot of old-timers around who really know the business, know the company."

The bright and comfortable conference room upstairs is a testament to past successes. David points out the handsome display of the Red Ryder,

recently celebrating its fiftieth year in production with an explosion of increased sales, and explains the success and importance of the company's shooting education kits, made up of programs and competitions co-sponsored with the United States Jaycees. He demonstrates how heavy the adult power-line air rifle is, and excitedly tells of the manufacture of firearms, "a brand-new thing for Daisy," since only toy guns and airguns were made there before. The new line, he says, being extremely competitive with other brands because of its low price and collection of unique features, should shoot Daisy way ahead in a new market.

"We feel free to say bigger," David says of Daisy's future. "We're growing now, and we have every intention of getting bigger. If all we could do was stay the same size, we'd not be very happy with ourselves."

Photographs on these pages were taken in the locations referenced on map.

1. *Arkansas City, p. 54*
2. *Ozark Mountains, pp. 56-57*
3. *Stuttgart, pp. 58, 59*
4. *Little Rock, p. 60*
5. *Searcy, p. 61*
6. *Russellville, p. 62*
7. *North Little Rock, p. 63*
8. *Altus, pp. 64, 65*
9. *Little Rock, p. 66*

Qualities, visions, and stories of hard work like these exemplify the zest of our state's work face. Be they bankers, lawyers, teachers, or factory workers, Arkansas workers have a dedication to and pride in their endeavors that makes the difference in the state. Newer, more high-tech operations—Systematics, Inc., a data processing and software company in Little Rock, and Acxiom Corporation, a conglomerate of direct marketing and information companies based in Conway, for example—are finding that these qualities add to their successes as well.

People account for the high quality of products and services manufactured in Arkansas. Individuals working together are the reason the state produces everything from color television sets to communication equipment, from boats to aircraft components. Add fine-tasting wines, stretch limousines, and reams and reams of paper to the list as well.

Every year new industries are settling in the state, new services are being provided, farmers are learning new techniques, and the legislature and related agencies are working to provide an ever-improving business climate. Arkansas has indeed been a land of opportunity for many individuals, families, and companies, and it should be for many more in years to come.

Set amidst signs of progress, the Old State House reminds Arkansans of their heritage.

Small manufacturing plants provide jobs throughout the state. (Courtesy of Arkansas Industrial Development Commission.)

Skilled horseshoers are kept busy in a state where horse racing and equestrian activities abound.

A Sample Menu of Arkansas Products

The production of rice and other food products is to be expected in a state as rich in agriculture as Arkansas. The same can be said for lumber and paper goods, since so much of the state is covered in forests. And it's not surprising that boats and fishing gear are manufactured within our water-abundant state.

But here are a few things you might not expect to be made in Arkansas:

Thermostats at White-Rodgers, Division of Emerson Electronics, Batesville.

Lariat rope at Dub Grant Lariat Rope, Benton.

Marble vanity tops at NWA Marble Mfg. Co., Inc., Bentonville.

Plastic and rubber combs at Ace Comb Company, Booneville.

Night lights at Nite Lite Company, Clarksville.

School buses at American Transportation Company, Conway.

Grand pianos at Baldwin Piano and Organ Company, Conway.

Plumes for band uniforms at Ligon Company, Inc., Conway.

Pool and snooker tables at Corning Pool Table Company, Corning.

Dog brushes at Warner Products, DeQueen.

Disposable diapers at Chicopee, East Camden.

Electric cable at Amercable, El Dorado.

Electronic body fat calculators at Caldwell, Justiss & Company, Inc., Fayetteville.

Handlebar grips at Johar Industrial/Sports Products Division, Forrest City.

Limousines at Henry Brothers, Inc., Manila.

Model airplane motors at Fox Manufacturers, Fort Smith.

Skylights at American Dynamics, Harrison.

Parking meters at Duncan Industries, Harrison, and POM, Inc., Russellville.

Loudspeaker systems at Klipsch & Associates, Inc., Hope.

The trucking industry is one of the fastest-growing businesses in the state.

Rubber bands at Alliance Rubber Company, Hot Springs.

Bottled mineral spring water at Diamond Water, Inc., Hot Springs, and at Mountain Valley Springs Company, Hot Springs.

Home exercise equipment at Continental Systems, Jonesboro.

Silk flowers at American Prestige, Inc., Little Rock.

Whirlpool baths at Jacuzzi Brothers Division, Little Rock.

Street and parking lot sweepers at Aaplex, Inc., Maumelle.

Automatic dog feeders at O.D. Funk Manufacturing, Inc., North Little Rock.

Electric shopping carts at Sage Industries, Rogers.

Golf clubs at Aristocrat Products, Inc., Siloam Springs.

Water meters at Rockwell International Corp., Measurement and Control Division, Texarkana.

TALENT

Old-time music is performed by members of the Rackensack Folklore Society.

Looking for talent in Arkansas is somewhat like searching for tomatoes on a vine. First you see the ripest, the ones that stand out as exceptional. Then, without even trying, you realize there are many more. Some may only be beginning to show the marks of maturity and others only hinting at their potential, but they are there. So it is with talent. Singers, athletes, actors, sculptors, writers, musicians, painters—Arkansas has them all.

Only in the last half-century, though, has the state had the money or time to take much official interest in these gifted individuals. Since the 1950s, the University of Arkansas Razorbacks athletic teams have captured the loyalty of the state, and cultural events have attracted greater attention than ever before.

Arkansans have always held athletic ability in great esteem. It stands to reason that in a state settled through rugged physical effort, skill in this area would be something to admire. The state's schools naturally have been the training grounds for many of the state's finest athletes. Coaching and practice have paid off for many youngsters who have worked and sweated their way through the ranks of junior and senior high school sports to receive scholarships to take part in college athletics.

In addition to the Razorbacks, the University of Arkansas at Little Rock

Joseph Kelly has established DMZ, the Readings, a coffeehouse for literary and performing arts in Little Rock.

Trojans have won the loyalty of central Arkansas basketball fans with their many top performances, while the Arkansas State University Indians have won title after title to the delight of eastern Arkansans. Members of the Arkansas Intercollegiate Conference dazzle crowds with skillful performances in swimming and track as well. No wonder the state has sent her share of these talented individuals on to star in the national limelight—baseball great Kevin McReynolds, and basketball dazzler Sidney Moncrief, for instance.

Arkansas's athletic prowess is fast rising in ranks in competitive swimming as well. In 1988, eleven swim-mers from the Little Rock Racquet Club Dolphins represented Arkansas in the men's Olympic trials. Only four teams, all from long-standing swim programs, had more qualifying competitors. Arkansas's strong showing produced a "What-the-heck-are-you-guys-doing-down-there?" reaction from the rest of the country, according to Dolphin coach Paul Blair.

The answer is quite simple. They are following through on a goal established in 1962 by a group of parents who wanted their children to have the chance to reach nationally competitive status as swimmers or tennis players. Several years, coaches, and dollars

Arkansas Razorback players practice before a game while fans fill the stands at War Memorial Stadium at Little Rock.

later, the Little Rock Racquet Club was producing swimmers such as Tom Genz, who competed in the 1984 United States Olympic Trials. And the number of national titles the swim team brings home each year has been increasing steadily.

Since 1958, the Arkansas Sports Hall of Fame has been honoring Arkansas's finest athletes. Sports heroes like Little Rock native Brooks Robinson, who for twenty-three years manned third base for the Baltimore Orioles, and Crossett native Barry Switzer, former Arkansas Razorback and longtime winning coach for the University of Oklahoma Sooners, now are immortalized within the annals of Arkansas sports.

Award-winning coach Harold Horton has produced many victorious teams at the University of Central Arkansas at Conway. (Courtesy of University of Central Arkansas.)

Coach Mike Newell has transformed the little-known University of Arkansas at Little Rock Trojans into a nationally recognized basketball team. (Courtesy of University of Arkansas at Little Rock.)

In addition to the deep-seated love for athletics, the quest for culture and the support of artistic talent in Arkansas has been growing at a remarkable rate. The interest seems to be late-blooming, but "Arkansas is a very young state—young not only in existence but young in wealth," Townsend Wolfe, executive director and chief curator of the Arkansas Arts Center in Little Rock, says. Especially considering her young age, the state has much to boast about in the arts arena. The visual arts, theater, opera, ballet, and symphonies are thriving statewide.

The Arkansas Arts Center, for example, was founded in 1961. In addition to hosting around twenty-two exhibits a year—juried regional art shows, traveling exhibits on loan from major institutions, and special-medium shows—the institution conducts a vigorous schedule of adult and children's art classes and sends works touring outside Little Rock in its "Artmobile." According to Wolfe, almost 400,000 men, women, and children come to the arts center annually. "They're used to coming here and used to being challenged (by the quality and depth of the art) and they're not offended by it any more. And that's very important. . . . If you get offended you're going to pull down that (mental) curtain and you're not going to get any further."

One decision made early on in the life of the Arkansas Arts Center has proven exceedingly wise. Because works on paper are less expensive than canvases, but equally valuable in terms of aesthetics and scholarship, Wolfe and his board decided to emphasize works on paper in their museum acquisitions. As a result, the arts center now has an outstanding reputation for its collection of works on paper, which numbers 1,500 of its total permanent collection of 7,000. In fact, in 1988 Wolfe was selected special curator of a collection of American drawings to represent the United States at an exhibit in Paris. "People found out in

Townsend Wolfe, executive director of the Arkansas Arts Center, has put together a nationally acclaimed collection of American drawings as well as an impressive library.

The resident dalmation appears to be one of the works of art at Urbi et Orbi, a Little Rock gallery.

Thousands of visitors attend the Arkansas Folk Festival, yet quiet moments can still be had.

Washington," Wolfe said, "and they had courage enough to ask someone from Arkansas to do it."

That same challenge of increasing quality art in the state is what attracted Robert Henderson to the job of directing the Arkansas Symphony Orchestra. "It was a chance to do things not only on a musical level, but on other levels, because they really didn't have the organization," he says. The group of musicians Henderson found when he came in the early 1980s "was basically an emerging orchestra that started under amateur auspices, as most orchestras do. . . . There was much about this orchestra that was social when I got here, and my goal was to change that as much as I could to professional."

He's been able to do that. Today's widely acclaimed orchestra consists of some musicians who have played with the ASO since its early days; others who once had to leave Arkansas in order to play professionally, but took advantage of the chance to come back home and do so; and others recently graduated from some of the best music schools in the country. Henderson points out that the Arkansas Symphony Orchestra has one of the largest followings of any comparably ranked orchestra in the United States. "Robinson Auditorium seats about 2,600 people, and for most metropolitan orchestras, about 2,600 is what they can count on on any concert weekend. Well, we play pairs [of concerts] because our audience is too large—we play to about 4,000." The demanding performance schedule includes six classical concerts, three pops concerts, two outdoor summer concerts, and

fifteen state touring events every season. In addition Arkansas audiences are treated to frequent concerts by subgroups of the full orchestra—the Arkansas Chamber Orchestra and a number of small ensembles.

Richard Steinert too was pleasantly surprised with the talent he found when he came to Ballet Arkansas to interview for the position of artistic director in 1986. Somewhat skeptical about the prospective job, the experienced dancer "came to meet with the [BA] board and to see the company, and honestly—and I say this honestly, this is no hype—I was really impressed with the dancers. . . . I was real pleased. The training [the dancers had had] was quite nice." Ballet Arkansas leaped to a new era in 1988 when, for the first time, it hired eight full-time, professional dancers. Until then, its company had consisted of students at its academy as well as a few part-time professionals. Now part-time dancers are still brought in to augment the basic company in the ballet's busy schedule of four annual performances in Little Rock and frequent lecture-demonstrations and performances elsewhere in the state.

Support for the fine arts is growing so much that many arts organizations have had to arrange for new facilities. The growth of the Arkansas Repertory Theater, for instance, has necessitated two moves within twelve years to accommodate its ever-larger audiences. Founded in the mid-1970s in a small space next to a Little Rock neighborhood ice cream shop, the Arkansas Rep, as it's dubbed, moved a few years later to a vacant church building. In 1988, the theater's strong following demanded yet another new location, this one a renovated building in downtown Little Rock. In addition to having an orchestra pit, a feature the Arkansas Rep never had before, and an expansive backstage, the new house can seat an audience of more than 350, three times more than before. More theatergoers than ever can enjoy the professionally staged comic, experimental, musical, and dramatic fare that the Rep offers year-round.

Choral groups, literary organizations, improv companies, opera, live readings—they can't all be described here. But the optimistic news about the fine arts in Arkansas continues.

Photographs on these pages were taken in the locations referenced on map.

Bill Beard plays his fiddle during a city festival.

During the early years of our statehood, energies and available monies were by necessity devoted to those basic, more pragmatic items needed for everyday life. So for years many of the artistic pieces made by Arkansans were utilitarian in nature. Quilts, candles, furniture, and other items were all made, often quite beautifully, simply to be used.

What happened as a result was that Arkansas was late to invest in pieces for their aesthetic worth alone. Bev Lindsey, director of the Arkansas Arts Council, says, "It took a long time for Arkansas to realize and capitalize on the heritage of the Ozarks. It had always been portrayed as the Hatfields and McCoys, the hillbillies. And it's hard, when you live with it and you try to outgrow that image all your life, to

recognize that it does have . . . impact on your cultural and on your public awareness."

Indeed these art forms are a rich part of our cultural past, present, and future. Luckily, many of them are being celebrated through organizations such as the Rackensack Folklore Society. Formed in the early 1960s, Rackensack seeks to preserve the folk songs and music of the country's past, and to entertain as it does so. The attempt is made to reproduce the music as it was originally played; that means no electric guitars, pianos, amplifiers, or drums. The society's growing numbers, and the ever-increasing audiences at their shows, indicate an increased awareness of and appreciation for this aspect of the state's heritage.

The Ozark Folk Center at Mountain

View is another place where the traditional arts and a down-home spirit live on. The center, one of the state's major tourist attractions, is a place where crafts like basketmaking, woodcarving, knife making, and spinning once again are being practiced and taught, and their worth demonstrated to younger generations. A number of artists have been able to make a living practicing their crafts at the folk center.

Potters David and Becki Dahlstedt have helped preserve a tradition while doing what they like best—shaping and decorating clay. David studied pottery at Henderson State University in Arkadelphia and then worked in a pottery shop in Hot Springs before going to work at the folk center. Becki, on the other hand, studied just about every other visual art form besides pottery at

Southeast Missouri State University, realizing only years later her enchantment with the special demands and possibilities of clay.

That integral combination of technique and artistry appeals most to the husband and wife team, who met, appropriately enough, at the folk center. "I like a lot of the engineering and designing aspects of making functional pots—pitchers, teapots—pots that actually perform the function that they're intended to and look nice while they're doing it," David explains. "So you can be real creative but also there's a nice tradition that's secure as long as you've got the skills to express that tradition."

Becki initially viewed pottery "as just another surface to paint on," and she still loves air brushing and experimenting with different colors and consistencies of glazes. But she also values the basic formative techniques that must be mastered. "As much as my skill will allow me to do, I can do with the clay," she explains, "so it's a challenge to really improve your skill. It's like if I want a nice, big vase to paint on, I've got to be able to make a nice, big vase."

Whether pottery should be classified as an art or a craft is an ongoing debate, David said. The line between functional and aesthetic purposes may be artificial. David probably speaks for a lot of artists when he says, "I don't know what the value of either of those designations is, really. A good sound craft is just as valid to me as fine art."

Works by Arkansas artists are showing up in an increasing number of galleries, arts centers, public exhibits, and private collections. The Arkansas Arts Council has played a valuable role in this invigorating period of awareness of Arkansas talents. "I think one of the most important things we can do at this agency is to work with other Arkansas government agencies that deal with either business development or with marketing the state or with tourism," Lindsey says, noting that her organization can "help provide outlets for the

An Ozark Folk Center staff member packages herbs.

A blacksmith at Old Washington State Park shows off the famous "Arkansas Toothpick," the Bowie knife David Bowie had made there on his way to the Alamo in the 1840s.

work both in state and out of state." The council also gives grant money each year to arts organizations and individual artists.

"We're trying to give support to the communities so they themselves can have a better choice in what programming they participate in," Lindsey explains, and "to provide support to individual artists to encourage them to stay in Arkansas, to live here and work here and to continue their progress and advancement."

Indeed, many artists have found working in Arkansas a mixed blessing. They elect to locate here "because of the natural environments offered by the state, since it's a nice place to live and you don't have the high costs here that are involved if you go to the larger cities where you have a more viable arts community," in Lindsey's opinion. Yet she adds, "It's difficult for artists to market their works outside of the state"—although she believes this situation is slowly turning around.

Richard DeSpain, well known for his ability to reproduce Arkansas sites and scenes in remarkably accurate pen-and-ink drawings, has enjoyed living and working in Arkansas all his life. Yet he knows all too well the frustration that comes with struggling to have his work appreciated in his home state. In fact, when he is away from his regular "day job" as an artist with the Cooperative Extension Service, he spends much of his time delivering or showing his work to local art galleries. "In Arkansas there're not enough people buying art" to support his pen and pencil habit, he says, adding that "art is not something that's going to feed you or keep you warm. It's more of a pleasure thing."

Yet he has built up a strong market of DeSpain collectors here, so the artist says he wouldn't think of uprooting and starting over elsewhere. Besides, he enjoys and is dedicated to what he does, often spending six to eight hours a night working on a drawing. "I feel like if

I'm going to make the most of my productive years with my eyesight still being fairly decent, then I've got to, as they say, make hay while the sun shines." And with a portfolio containing more than 250 black and white pen-and-inks and more than 15 watercolors (a relatively new medium for DeSpain), no one could argue that he has not been doing that.

While he has toyed with different styles, he's found what he likes best is very detailed, extremely precise drawing. His works are often so realistic that they are mistaken for photographs. "That's why I'd rather do more line-work drawing that pointillism or dots," he said, "because the dots tend to look like a blown-up photograph, and I don't want them to look like that." But he does like for his art to look real, "to capture a moment in time. . . . Everybody's got a will to do that, to want to catch a certain something in time and preserve it." Some of the things DeSpain has preserved for future viewers are Little Rock's skyline, the Old State House Museum, Victorian buildings in Eureka Springs, and scenes of Oaklawn Park at Hot Springs. "I want a person . . . to be able to look at that and say, 'Yeah, that's exactly how it is,'" DeSpain says of his work.

Many other artists who call Arkansas home find a wealth of raw material here to mold and shape in their own particular medium. Photographer Andrew Kilgore, for instance, has put together powerful collections of stark portraits, many of native Arkansans. With nothing but a backdrop to distract from the intense study of an individual's facial expression and body gestures, Kilgore's photographs capture the complexity of each individual. Author Joan Hess has woven many a spunky mystery using characters very similar to people living and working here. And on television's

Dee Brown, an Arkansas native and resident, has penned many works of fiction and non-fiction, including **Bury My Heart at Wounded Knee.**

"Designing Women," producer Harry Thomason and his Missouri-born wife, Linda Bloodworth-Thomason, have characterized Southerners—Arkansans included—in a much more flattering and realistic vein than is the network norm.

Dee Brown, most famous for his book *Bury My Heart at Wounded Knee,* is one of the state's accomplished talents who has chosen to live here. "There are

some places I like better than Arkansas. . . . In none of them, however, do I feel that I am home. I like them, but they are not truly part of me. Arkansas is a part of me, and there is nothing I could do about it, and probably would not if I could," Brown once wrote in an essay for the *Arkansas Gazette.* He now says that the small size and historic poverty of Arkansas sometimes make the state "seem like a Third

Political cartoonist George Fisher is recognized nationally for his observations of local, state, national, and world affairs.

Cliff Baker, in the middle of the auditorium of the Arkansas Repertory Theatre, directs activity on stage.

World country, but it's *my* Third World country." Brown, who has nearly thirty books to his credit, has written both fiction and non-fiction. Western novels are a particular trademark, resulting from the fact that "when I was a boy there were no space books and very little science fiction—Western books, that's what we read." And despite his uncanny ability to create colorful fictional characters, the central incidents in such books of Brown's as *Showdown at Little Bighorn* or the Civil War adventure *Conspiracy of Knaves* never depart from fact. "I try to be true to history," Brown explains, and that

means never having "some real person who's named in the book—say Andrew Jackson is in the book, I wouldn't have him out in the Rocky Mountains. You don't jerk people around and have them in situations they couldn't be in."

But fiction, even of the historical variety, isn't Brown's favorite mode of writing. In fact, the book he enjoyed working on most was *The Year of the Century: 1876*. The hours spent in libraries across the country poring through old magazines and newspapers "gave me great pleasure," he says.

Other Arkansas notables are Academy Award–winning actress Mary

Steenburgen, who grew up in North Little Rock and has found fame in Hollywood, and widely acclaimed opera singer Susan Dunn, a native of Bauxite, who has sung before audiences at Milan's La Scala and with the Chicago Lyric Opera. And names like country singer Glen Campbell, actors Gil Gerard and Frank Bonner, writers Charles Portis and Jack Butler, cartoonist George Fisher, and musician Levon Helm all have an Arkansas ring.

Arkansans need not be afraid their store of talent is running low, either. One only has to attend a performance of the Arkansas Children's Theater or one of the youth orchestras, a high school track meet, a Little League baseball game, or a rehearsal of the Ballet Arkansas Dance Academy to realize that. And colleges and universities offer almost daily proof of the state's great store of talent with all kinds of performances and athletic events.

Truly this is an exciting time to pursue one's talents in Arkansas. The mounting enthusiasm for what is being done, and what can be done, is contagious, and it provides a stimulating atmosphere not only for those with special gifts in artistic and athletic fields but for those who simply enjoy and appreciate the riches these talents produce.

Craig Fuller applies make-up before a production at the Arkansas Repertory Theatre in Little Rock.

LOCAL ARTS ORGANIZATIONS

Participation in the arts is widespread and abundant in Arkansas, as shown by the following list of arts organizations:*

Folk whimsey by an unknown artist decorates the landscape near Clinton.

Arkansas Arts Center, Little Rock
Arkansas Blues Connection, Little Rock
Arkansas Chamber Singers, Little Rock
Arkansas Choral Society, Little Rock
Arkansas Country Dance Society, Little Rock
Arkansas Dance Theatre, Little Rock
Arkansas Jazz Society, Trumann
Arkansas League of Artists, statewide group
Arkansas Opera Theatre, Little Rock
Arkansas Repertory Theatre, Little Rock
Arkansas River Valley Arts Center, Russellville
Arkansas Songwriters Association, statewide group
Arkansas Symphony Orchestra, Little Rock
Arkadelphia Community Theater, Arkadelphia
Art Center of the Ozarks, Springdale
Art League of Crossett, Crossett
Arts and Science Center of Southeast Arkansas, Pine Bluff
Arts Council of Conway County, Morrilton
Arts Live!, Fayetteville
Back Porch Players, Stuttgart
Ballet Arkansas, Little Rock
Batesville Community Theatre, Batesville
Batesville Symphony League, Batesville
Blytheville Fine Arts Council, Blytheville
Cabot Fine Arts Council, Cabot
Cleburne County Arts Council, Heber Springs
Community Arts of Conway, Conway
Community Theatre of Camden, Camden
Community Theatre of Little Rock, Little Rock
Corning Art Association, Corning
Crawford County Arts Center, Van Buren
Crittenden Fine Arts Center, West Memphis
Cross County Fine Arts Council, Wynne
Crossett Players, Inc., Crossett
DMZ, The Readings, Little Rock
Dumas Community Theater, Dumas
Fairfield Bay Fine Arts Council, Fairfield Bay
Fairfield Bay Little Theatre, Fairfield Bay
Fayetteville/University of Arkansas Arts Center Council, Fayetteville
Foothills Li'l Theatre, Ozark
Fort Smith Arts Center, Fort Smith
Fort Smith Chorale, Fort Smith
Fort Smith Community Children's Theatre, Fort Smith
Fort Smith Little Theatre, Fort Smith

The Foundation of the Arts, Jonesboro
Gentry Fine Arts Society, Gentry
Grand Prairie Arts Council, Stuttgart
Greene County Fine Arts Council, Paragould
Hempstead County Arts Council, Hope
Hot Springs Arts Center, Hot Springs
I Believe in McGehee, McGehee
Joint Educational Consortium, Arkadelphia
King Opera House Players, Van Buren
Magnolia Arts Council, Magnolia
Merely Players, Yellville
Mid-Southern Watercolor Society, statewide group
Montgomery County Council for the Performing Arts, Mount Ida
Music Festival of Arkansas, Fayetteville
North Arkansas Council for Arts, Mountain Home
North Arkansas Symphony Society, Fayetteville
North Central Arkansas Concert Association, Harrison
North Little Rock Community Concert Band, North Little Rock
Ouachita Little Theatre, Mena
Our Town Players, Morrilton
Ozark Creative Writers, statewide group
Ozark Folk Center, Mountain View
Ozark Regional Craft Association, Mountain View
Patchwork Company, Calico Rock
Pine Bluff Symphony Orchestra, Pine Bluff
Pocahontas Fine Arts Council, Pocahontas
Poets Roundtable of Arkansas, statewide group
Russellville Community Symphony, Russellville
Porch City Players, Pine Bluff
Sager Creek Arts Center, Siloam Springs
Southeast Arkansas Concert of the Arts, Monticello
Spotlite Players, Monticello
South Arkansas Arts Center, El Dorado
South Arkansas Symphony, El Dorado
Strawberry River Arts Association, Horseshoe Bend
Teak Repertory Theatre, Little Rock
Texarkana Arts and History Council, Texarkana
The Theatre Company, Harrison
Trumann Fine Arts, Trumann
Twin Lakes Playhouse, Mountain Home
Warfield Concerts, Helena
Western Arkansas Ballet, Fort Smith
West Memphis Little Theatre, West Memphis
Words: The Arkansas Literary Society, statewide group

*Information courtesy of Arkansas Arts Council

A pastry chef creates edible works of art at Little Rock's Capital Hotel.

*The University of Arkansas at Little Rock
Law School occupies one of downtown Little
Rock's renovated historical buildings.*

EDUCATION

Young, questioning minds are perhaps the most valuable resource a state can have—the biggest responsibility, too. So it's no wonder that education is a major concern in Arkansas. During the early 1980s, Governor Bill Clinton pushed the issue to the fore of his political agenda. Since then, the challenge of providing the best education possible to every young Arkansan has become everyone's concern. Educators and business leaders have joined forces to provide new programs and to make existing ones more efficient. The general public has teamed up with school administrators and classroom teachers to improve local schools and the lives of their children as students.

While a good number of the state's best educational programs are a direct result of this renewed effort, many others were already in place. That's why learning adventures for everyone from the tiniest tot to the oldest senior citizen can be found here, many of them as exciting as they are effective. In Arkansas, experiences which broaden thoughts and strengthen minds don't happen only in the classroom. Not at all.

Much learning occurs long before a child reaches the door of her first-grade schoolroom. Head Start and Montessori school programs are offered in most areas of the state, and day-care centers and kindergartens are even more plentiful. One of the best exam-

A docent tells about lizards to visitors at the Little Rock Zoo.

Young children learn while playing at the First United Methodist Church Child Development Center in Little Rock.

State park interpreters at Woolly Hollow
State Park near Greenbrier demonstrate and
explain the skills, crafts, and tools of early
Arkansans.

ples of early childhood education can be found in downtown Little Rock at the First United Methodist Church Child Development Center.

Housed in a what once was a car dealership, the CDC's building is a colorful, stimulating place for small minds and bodies to grow. "I worked with the architect to design a building that would be specifically for children," says Cindy Thomas, the center's executive director. Color-coded doors help young ones recognize their "home base" when returning from lunch or recess, and the covered playground on the building's roof is creatively designed with chain-link walls that allow fresh air to blow through and garage doors that can enclose the area on cold days.

Yet the real draw of the place is the experience the children have there.

"My philosophy is that you cannot babysit a child without having some learning going on," Thomas says, adding that the approach at the center is to help children learn as much as they can without pushing them to do more than they're able. "Learning at a six-week-old level versus learning at a four-year-old level is a whole different kind of learning. But it's basically a hands-on learning" since pre-schoolers understand more that way. "Be it learning manners, science, health, songs, gymnastics, nursery rhymes, letter recognition," Thomas continues, "the key is to teach them with hands-on experiences." Providing quality day care for preschoolers, Thomas says, is a hot issue nationwide. "Now you're seeing more and more child care centers," she explains, "not just to meet the needs of the underprivileged—and that's really how it started out—but the working class, the upper class, are wanting and needing child care, so it's evolving into a

quality program across the nation." She points out the many benefits of a good day-care program, including socializing and structured learning skills. "There are so many [children] now in centers that those who aren't are almost disadvantaged, because they don't already have the advantage of knowing how to work in a group together" and haven't received the education those in day care programs have.

While elementary and junior and

senior high schools traditionally have been places for children to learn everything from reading and multiplying to diagramming sentences and performing trigonometric functions, that basic core of knowledge doesn't suffice anymore. Today's young person hungers for more cultural nourishment than that; at the same time, our technological society demands even broader skills.

Taking the fine arts to the schools is

one of the best ways to satisfy that need for cultural exposure. And the state's major arts organizations—the ballet, the symphony orchestra, theater troupes, and the opera—have done that by designing touring shows specifically for school-aged audiences. Whether it's the Arkansas Opera Theatre performing *The Night Harry Stopped Smoking* or the Arkansas Symphony Orchestra string quartet demonstrating the repertoire of a violin or cello, the exposure is an exciting and often unique treat for children. Ann Chotard, executive director of the Arkansas Opera Theatre, says productions are shown to students "not to get them into

opera, but (to create) an awareness that these things exist."

The Arts in Education Program, sponsored by the Arkansas Arts Council, is a more intensive effort to bring art into the lives of children. Bev Lindsey, executive director of the council, calls the program "an ideal situation. The students are involved with the conception and with the creation as well as the execution of the project. Sometimes it's fiction writing or poetry," but it can center on any kind of art form. The council gives out a number of grants each year to schools that propose stimulating projects. Usually the schools already know of an artist who will work

Children learn to express themselves by painting at the Arkansas Arts Center's Art Party in the Park. (Courtesy of Department of Parks and Tourism, photo by C.H. Pierce.)

with them. This artist—a painter, photographer, or writer, not an art teacher—spends a designated amount of time in the schools working with students on a piece of work.

In El Dorado, the Arts in Education program and artist Jorge Villegas are practically the same entity. Villegas, a native of Buenos Aires, Argentina, has been working with the AIE program in El Dorado since 1981, two years after he arrived in the country. "I saw the opportunity to go into the schools as an artist," says Villegas, a visual artist who also is certified to teach fine arts. "The schools have a great need for art in education. It's considered one of the basics."

Photographs on these pages were taken in the locations referenced on map.

1. *Little Rock, pp. 88-89*
2. *Little Rock, pp. 89, 90*
3. *Greenbrier, p. 91*
4. *Little Rock, p. 92*
5. *Little Rock, p. 93*

The University of Arkansas for Medical Sciences is the training ground for a number of medical professionals.

So Villegas spends each semester painting, drawing, making stained glass, or following wherever the muses lead him and his students. Each semester is spent at one of El Dorado's eight elementary schools, where, he says, "[I] work with the kids, work with the teachers, or whoever would like to get involved. We usually involve almost everybody. Even the cook was trying to paint or do something. It really generates a lot of good feeling and good energy."

Each project begins with a period of study and discussion. "The kids have to be motivated," Villegas explains. To do that, "We talk about a lot of things in order to come up with a project. When you talk to the kids, you introduce them to a cultural and new outlet, which is maybe art history or painters or [an art] movement, and after that they start to catch up with your ideas. So what the program does is, it broadens the cultural knowledge of the kids." He acts as facilitator by playing classical music while informing the students of the piece's composer, subject, and origin. Or he'll introduce them to painters like Picasso and Jackson Pollock and help them understand and imitate their styles.

The elementary schools in the oil-boom town are full of murals, stained-glass, paintings, and wall hangings—all of which look as though they were done by professionals, not pre-teens, and none of which was there before the program began. As one of the elementary school principals declares, "He's done neat work, and every one of our elementary schools shows it."

Villegas believes art provides children with a necessary creative outlet; it nurtures their emotional and spiritual growth by giving them productive modes of self-expression. "The idea of the Arts in Education program is not to produce artists. It tries to give the possibility to every individual, not just the gifted and talented kids, but to work with every individual and try to reach them with the ideas of art and cover the ideas of their cultures and civilizations."

He wholeheartedly believes in the AIE program because he has seen the results. "After you work with the kids—we're talking about kindergarten students through sixth-graders—on all the levels you see those kids develop. A sense of self-expression, a sense of caring for things like the weather or the trees or animals . . . in a sense for their own work, which is a sense of pride. They feel proud of their work, proud of what they're doing."

*A potter prepares his kiln for a firing at the
Ozark Folk Center in Mountain View.*

On the other end of the educational spectrum is the use of computers in the classroom. Computers are beginning to enhance learning in at least one school in every county; soon they will be present in every school. Project IMPAC (Instructional Microcomputer Project for Arkansas Classrooms), a productive marriage between private business and state government, is responsible for this growth of computer literacy in school-aged youth. So now while nine-year-olds at Marmaduke Elementary School are using computers to master the tough task of multiplying double-digit numbers, twelve-year-olds in North Little Rock's Rose City Junior High School are learning the components of sentences.

The project began in the early 1980s when a group of parents of public school students began to publicize the need for computer education. By 1983 they had made their case convincingly to school officials and the wider community. The most energetic response came from a group of Arkansas business people, who donated $250,000 for a school-based computer learning program to be run under their auspices. Soon the Arkansas Commission on Microcomputer Instruction, made up of business and education leaders appointed by the governor, was formed. The commission is closely linked to a separate, privately formed, nonprofit company; the unusual alliance allows Project IMPAC to have access to monies not provided by the state, yet still to work closely with the state Education Department.

Subiaco Academy, a school for boys for more than a century, stands majestically atop a hill in western Arkansas.

The University of Arkansas at Little Rock offers undergraduate and graduate degrees to students from around the world.

Strange as it sounds, learning to use computers is not the goal of Project IMPAC. Its aim, according to its director, Cecil McDermott, is "to help teachers teach students basic skills." Much-improved test scores among students involved in the program show that the goal is being met. McDermott believes that "the IMPAC program contributes to the improvement of basic skills probably in every program. It contributes more where the students are below average than it does where they're above average," he said, since it's harder to show gains when a student has already mastered much of the material.

By the turn of the century, McDermott envisions the use of computers in every school system in the state. Of course the programs for older students will be much more sophisticated, he said, and instead of focusing on basic skills they will be geared to any number of specific subject areas.

A wide variety of special learning opportunities for Arkansas teens exists outside the walls of the school building as well. Band and choir camps, environmental conferences, and a number of summer internships address specific interests; for example, the Arkansas Boys' State and Girls' State programs, sponsored by the American Legion, give high school juniors an up-close look at the workings of local, county, and state politics. Delegates to these week-long seminars elect representatives, senators, and other state officials up to governor, and all of them then get

to spend a day at the Capitol acting out their roles.

One of the most popular programs for high school students is the Arkansas Governor's School. Founded in 1980, the school is a pioneer in its own right, being one of only a handful in the country. It has earned tremendous respect nationwide, even spawning workshops on how to develop similar programs and a video explaining its worth.

But the most important thing about Governor's School is what it does for the students who spend five weeks of their final high school summer there. Colleen McKenna, a student at one of the first sessions of Governor's School, says, "it was probably the first time that I'd ever been in an educational experience that was isolated from everything else. So not only can you think—and you're taught to think critically and analytically—but you're also able to reflect on what's going on."

According to Dr. Bruce Haggard, director of the school for several years,

the aim is to stimulate students already classified as gifted and talented to develop intellectually. Up to four hundred boys and girls arrive at Hendrix College in Conway at the beginning of the summer, not sure exactly what kind of experience they're about to embark on. Haggard says some expect it to be a sort of summer camp, or, at worst, a residential summer school. Yet, he said, it's neither.

"It certainly is not to be an acceleration of high school, nor is it to be an anticipation of college," Haggard explains. Instead, it is a twenty-four-hour-a-day, intellectually stimulating environment where the participants "can carry on a level of conversation and think about ideas and issues, some of them that are just weird, some of them crazy . . . that they just can't try out in a society where there's pressure not to be different, not to be weird, and pressure not to study these issues or to take them too seriously."

McKenna says that "for once, it was a good thing to be able to think and to

High school students take a break during a summer session of Arkansas Governor's School at Hendrix College at Conway.

It's easy to imagine what education in early Arkansas was like when viewing the schoolhouse at the Agricultural Museum at Stuttgart.

want to learn. . . . I really learned the importance of an education at that point." A student in the language arts area of Governor's School, McKenna says her experiences that summer strongly influenced her choice of an academic career and inspired in her an unquenchable thirst for learning. Those kinds of results are not uncommon, according to Haggard. Students "should go away with some concrete intellectual gains. They should know more about the particular discipline they were selected in, especially in the theory of that discipline. They should know . . . something about the epistemology of that discipline—how do we know what it is that we know, and how do we gain knowledge." He also often sees some affective changes, such as "a deeper appreciation for culture, a deeper appreciation for the life of the mind. They should come out of here with a greater self-confidence, without arrogance; they should come out of here with a greater enthusiasm for trying to make a difference in their world."

Life after high school offers many very different paths to Arkansas students. A few go straight into the working world, while others enter the armed services. For the many who continue their education, opportunities are as plentiful as they are varied.

The state has close to twenty-five vocational and technical schools offering programs to help young adults specialize in a trade. These institutions are available to students just out of high school as well as those wanting further training in a certain area. Automotive body repair, cosmetology, data processing, and diesel mechanics are a few of the subjects taught.

Many graduates choose to attend a college or university, and, for those wanting to stay in state, there are quite a few from which to choose. The University of Arkansas at Fayetteville is the state's largest single university, educating nearly 14,000 students each year,

Ole Main, with its distinctive architecture, is a landmark at the University of Arkansas at Fayetteville.

Meadowcreek Project at Fox offers a unique learning experience in ecology and environmental issues.

and Arkansas State University at Jonesboro is the next largest with close to 9,000 in its enrollment. The opportunity for a small-campus experience is available too, with several of the state universities having student populations of lower than several thousand and several of the private institutions' enrollments being lower than that.

In addition to the on-campus opportunities for Arkansas college students, the isolated and spectacularly beautiful Meadowcreek Project—1,500 acres of hills, trees, and facilities located at Fox, in Stone County—offers a number of resident programs and internships for students specializing in environmental studies.

"We are not meant to be an alternative to college, but a supplement to it,"

said Dr. David Orr, director of educational and research programs and a founder of Meadowcreek. "Our primary target is upper division undergraduates and graduate students." Those students, who have backgrounds in any subject from agriculture to business and who represent not only Arkansas schools but colleges and universities all across the nation, come for a regular semester internship, a three-and-a-half-week "January term," and sometimes for no longer than a weekend conference to study environmental issues like resource management, renewable energy, and regenerative economics.

Meadowcreek students get to take a break from the normal academic setting since they do much of their study and research outdoors. A 300-acre farm, 1,100 acres of forest, solar energy fixtures, a woodshop, and a waste cycling process are some of the features of the Meadowcreek "classroom," which allows for the integration of hands-on, practical experience with the reading and discussing of related theories.

Any number of graduate and professional degrees can be earned in the state. There are two University of Arkansas law schools, one in Fayetteville and another in Little Rock. Masters and doctoral programs in many subject areas—mass communications, public administration, agricultural engineering, and comparative literature, just to name a few—are offered at several state institutions.

One of the most vital settings for graduate training is the University of Arkansas for Medical Sciences, which sprawls over several city blocks on West Markham Street in Little Rock. With a 450-bed teaching hospital and the Barton Research Institute, the five-college campus each year graduates well-qualified physicians, pharmacists, registered nurses and nurse practitioners, health care professionals, and scientists with advanced degrees in such

areas as anatomy, biochemistry, microbiology, and immunology. UAMS is a mecca of research as well, receiving large grants in recent years for the conducting of intense investigations—such as the school's Department of Ophthalmology's participation in a national study of optic neuritis, a common nerve disorder that causes severe vision loss; and pathology professor Dr. Richard Webber's research on ways to repair torn knee joints by learning about the biology of the menisci, the "shock absorbers" of the knee.

And one of the most exciting additions to the UAMS campus in the past few years is the Arkansas Cancer Research Center. Although ground for the building wasn't broken until 1987, the center had been in the dreaming stages years before that and in the actual planning and fundraising phases since 1984. The facility, a four-story, 50,000-square-foot structure, serves as a nucleus for oncologists and cancer researchers working together in a situation ideal for both individual investigation and cooperative effort. The hope for a cancer cure—an Arkansas-based one at that—is much closer to becoming a reality with the addition of the research facility.

A teacher instructs her young students with the help of computers.

Education is a lifelong adventure. Older, "non-traditional" students are increasingly heading back to the classroom, and several Arkansas schools also offer enticing continuing education classes that can be taken just for the fun of it. Art appreciation, folk dancing, and wine tasting are subjects that attract students of all ages and backgrounds.

Other special learning opportunities exist in a variety of settings and structures. The State Parks Service, for example, regularly offers informative seminars in outdoor amphitheaters, nature walks on rugged trails, and birdwatching weekends for those anxious to learn more about Arkansas's natural assets. Institutions such as the Leadership and Wilowe Institutes in Little Rock continually provide leadership training to professional, public- and civic-minded citizens. Classes in sewing, cooking, and general household management are offered on a regular basis through Home Extension Offices, while the state Farm Bureau and Cooperative Extension Service provide the latest agricultural methods and research findings to the state's farm population. YWCAs and YMCAs, churches, libraries, and other institutions from the Museum of Science and History to the Arkansas Endowment for the Humanities offer courses and services to enhance the quality of many facets of life.

The pursuit of truth and knowledge may seem to be a lofty ideal, but in Arkansas it is a valued one. Self-improvement as well as the knowledge and ability to make a contribution to the society we live in are motivating factors. What's more, the opportunities to pursue that ideal obviously are here.

Names of graduates of years gone by are etched into the Ole Main sidewalk at the University of Arkansas.

FOUR-YEAR COLLEGES AND UNIVERSITIES

So you want to teach school. Or design buildings. Or practice medicine. Everyone knows a career begins with a college degree, and in Arkansas there are a number of reputable institutions at which to earn one. Both state and private schools offer a variety of educational programs in a number of settings.

The colleges and universities in Arkansas are:

Arkansas Baptist College at Little Rock, with an enrollment of 225 and six baccalaureate degree programs.

Arkansas College at Batesville, with an enrollment of 700 and 24 baccalaureate degree programs.

Arkansas State University at Jonesboro, with an enrollment of 8,525 and 72 baccalaureate degree programs.

Arkansas Tech University at Russellville, with an enrollment of 3,275 and 44 baccalaureate degree programs.

Central Baptist College at Conway, with an enrollment of 225 and five baccalaureate degree programs.

Harding University at Searcy, with an enrollment of 2,775 and 80 baccalaureate degree programs.

Hendrix College at Conway, with an enrollment of 1,000 and 27 baccalaureate degree programs.

Henderson State University at Arkadelphia, with an enrollment of 2,950 and 47 baccalaureate degree programs.

John Brown University at Siloam Springs, with an enrollment of 850 and 21 baccalaureate degree programs.

Ouachita Baptist University at Arkadelphia, with an enrollment of 1,200 and 49 baccalaureate programs.

Philander Smith College at Little Rock, with an enrollment of 600 and 23 baccalaureate degree programs.

Southern Arkansas State University at Magnolia, with an enrollment of 2,050 and 43 baccalaureate degree programs.

Southern Baptist College at Walnut Ridge, with an enrollment of 475 and three bachelor degree programs.

University of Arkansas at Fayetteville, with an enrollment of 13,850 and 97 baccalaureate degree programs.

University of Arkansas at Little Rock, with an enrollment of 9,950 and 53 baccalaureate degree programs.

University of Arkansas for Medical Sciences at Little Rock, with an enrollment of 1,350 and six baccalaureate degree programs.

University of Arkansas at Monticello, with an enrollment of 1,850 and 37 degree programs.

University of Arkansas at Pine Bluff, with an enrollment of 2,900 and 44 baccalaureate degree programs.

University of Central Arkansas at Conway, with an enrollment of 6,425 and 65 baccalaureate degree programs.

University of the Ozarks at Clarksville, with an enrollment of 675 and 39 baccalaureate degree programs.

Little Rock's Central High School, widely respected for its educational offerings, graduates some of the state's top students each year.

*Sunrise finds fishermen already in their
boats on Harris Brake Lake.*

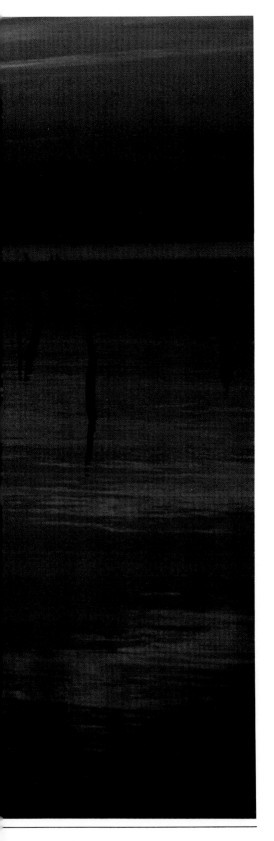

RECREATION

Arkansans have the pleasure of living in a virtual playground. With lakes, rivers, and mountains as their toys, they would find it hard to imagine a better place to frolic in the outdoors. And as if one couldn't find enough to do on one's own here—from playing volleyball on a sandy river beach, to camping deep in the woods, to rock climbing on a rugged mountainside—the state Parks and Tourism Department puts out a calendar of events listing enough year-round activities to boggle the mind.

Thoughts of outdoor recreation in Arkansas used to conjure up visions of burly men taking to the woods with rifles or children sitting on a bank with a fishing line dangling in the water, and to some extent those images hold true today. "Hunting is a very longstanding and deep tradition in Arkansas," Jim Low of the Arkansas Game and Fish Commission admits, "and fishing is more popular than any form of hunting." He adds that during each year in the 1980s, an average of over forty percent of the state's citizens hunted or

fished, a figure "higher than any but in six other states."

The proverbial thrill of the chase is of course part of hunting's appeal, not to mention the great taste of the reward

Eureka Springs, with its distinctive architecture and unique flavor, draws thousands of visitors each year.

when it's cooked up just right. But that's not the only excitement. After all, not just "he-men" take to the wild outdoors when hunting season opens.

Wild game, many sportsmen and women have found, isn't the only prize that hunting yields, for a special camaraderie develops within a group of friends when they spend a weekend at deer camp, drinking beer and telling stories to impress each other while outside the wind is howling and the temperature is dropping. And the same can be said for a parent and child who get to spend time together, sharing an adventure that both will remember and treasure.

Arkansas, with so much of its land still covered with forests, is good hunting ground indeed. Small game is ample all over the state; duck hunters should look to sites in the eastern delta region; and bear hunters need to search in the opposite direction, in the "designated bear zones" of the Ozark and Ouachita mountains. Deer hunters, probably the largest single group of hunters in the state, can find their prey in all areas of the state. Deer are most

Jogging and golfing are only two of the abundant choices for recreation in Arkansas.

This city park at Chester offers an ideal refuge on a fall day.

Cleaning fish, part of a day's work for any serious fisherman, marks the end of the day at a resort on the Little Red River.

Boating is a favorite summer activity on any of Arkansas's waterways.

Canoes are left to dry on the shores of the Buffalo River.

abundant in southern Arkansas, but according to Low the healthiest and biggest thrive in the Ozark Mountains.

Fishing is bound to be popular in a state where more than a quarter of the population owns fishing licenses. In fact, the activity "is the most frequently engaged in sport next to swimming," Low said. And no wonder. Arkansans can cast hook, line, and sinker into more than 9,000 miles of streams and 500,000 acres of lakes. And the fish most often pulled out of those waters are bass—largemouth bass in particular. Crappie and bream are also popular catches.

Trout fishing in the state's rivers and streams, though, isn't just recreation; it's business. Since the breed is not native to Arkansas, quite a bit of money is put into keeping the sport alive for Arkansas fishermen. Federal and state hatcheries supply over two million trout a year for the state's rivers and streams, Low says, a supply plentiful enough to allow the fish to grow to record-breaking size. Literally. In the fall of 1988, a world-record 38-pound, 12-ounce trout was pulled out of the White River.

There's no doubt that the quality of fishing in Arkansas is superb, and a number of professional fishing guides are available to take visitors to prime spots on lakes and rivers.

The abundant water that makes fishing so attractive to outdoor enthusiasts appeals to other sports lovers as well. Swimming, of course, is as natural as walking for many who live in Arkansas, but in addition "there's a tremendous amount of real high-quality water-related recreation available to the people," according to Frank Barton. Barton, owner of the Take a Hike outdoor supply stores in Little Rock, not only keeps up with outdoor trends but is involved in many of these sports himself.

Just as snowskiing is almost second nature in cold, mountainous states like Washington and Colorado, waterskiing

*North Arkansas's Bull Shoals Lake offers
fun for all ages.*

has scads of devotees in Arkansas. The sport has been around as long as boats have been equipped with power motors, and when the Corps of Engineers started building large, open lakes in the state it evolved into a high-tech pastime. It's hard to believe that at one time Arkansas skiers were pulled up and down rivers on homemade wooden skis behind small fishing boats. Now slalom and trick skis, specially designed ski boats, and all the accessories a waterskier could want are commonplace.

Yet, Barton says, "we are seeing more and more interest in non-motorized sports" in recent years. "I think people are discovering that people-powered equipment is a lot more fun, a lot more rewarding." So in addition to power boating, other types of craft are taking to the waters as well.

Canoes and kayaks, for instance, are two types of boats that recently have tested high and low waters both. Barton pointed to the development of the Buffalo River in northern Arkansas as a national river in the late '60s, along with the improvement and streamlining in

canoe construction in recent decades, as the real impetus for "this explosion of interest." Indeed, the Buffalo River is an ideal stream to paddle—its long stretches of calm, smooth water interrupted by just enough rapids to make the ride exciting.

While water sports are usually considered summer activities, canoeing and kayaking actually are best done in the early spring or late fall. Since more rain falls during that part of the year, rivers are higher and much more fun to float. And cool air shouldn't be a deterrent to boaters. "With modern wetsuits and dry suits, it can be done real comfortably [all winter long]," Barton says, "and that's a nice time to be out because all the foliage is off the trees and you can see all the rock formations and usually see some wildlife."

The rolling, splashing, breaking whitewater in streams like the Mulberry, the Big Piney, Illinois Bayou, and Little Missouri River beckon experienced canoeists to their rapids, but perhaps the most challenging in the state is the Cossatot. "I've paddled the Colorado through the Grand Canyon,"

Duck calling comes in handy in Arkansas's delta, the duck hunting capital of the world. (Courtesy of Department of Parks and Tourism.)

Barton says, "and when the Cossatot is high, it's just as difficult as anything in the Grand Canyon. Just spectacular. Most people who've never seen it, when they've laid eyes on it, they can't believe it's in Arkansas."

Sailing and, more recently, windsurfing, are two other sports that let Arkansans have fun in the water. Sailing clubs flourish here, and lakes like Greers Ferry, Ouachita, Maumelle, and De-Gray are favorites of sailors, whether they're rocking along in a small two-seater or cruising smoothly in a motor-propelled yacht-sized craft. Sailing is seasonal in Arkansas, best in the gusty months of March, April, and early May and October, November, and early December.

Windsurfing is probably the newest kid on the watersports block, Barton says. The activity is "still growing . . . but it's an excellent sport that's available to people." And with windsurfing, "we're capable of sailing in a lot higher winds than boats are, so when they issue wind warnings on the lakes, that's when we head out." The sport is quite rigorous; nevertheless, Barton says, it is suited for "anybody from a youngster that's barely big enough to hold a [sail-board's] rig to grandmas and grandpas."

Backpackers and hikers also have a heyday in Arkansas. Arkansas scenery makes these treks beautiful and peaceful. The Ouachita Trail, which originates near Little Rock and winds through the mountains west into Oklahoma, is a hiker's paradise. Other excellently marked trails that allow an escape from the fast pace of everyday life are the Caney Creek Back Country Trail, in southwest Arkansas, and the Ozark Highlands Trail, which stretches across the north central part of the state.

Arkansans frequently spend an hour, day, or even a week on a hiking excursion. In fact, Barton says, "there have been quite a few people who have made a project out of walking the length of these trails—that's not an

Boats on Lake Maumelle bob quietly in the morning fog.

Whitewater rapids offer a challenge to adventuresome kayakers and canoeists.

The wide, open fields and skies of eastern Arkansas are ideal for remote-controlled airplane enthusiasts.

uncommon activity." Some hardy souls have even been known to take their full two- or three-week vacation from work and spend it meandering and camping along the trails: for them, the perfect getaway. Because of our hot summers, October to March is probably the best time to take to the trails. The transitional seasons have their own spectacles, and wintertime offers the same rewards to hikers that it does to winter canoeists—the leaves already have fallen from the trees, allowing views of valleys and mountains that stretch to the horizon, bare rock strata, and every now and then a wild animal or two.

Those preferring to drive to and from their campsites are in luck too. Besides the forty-four state parks, where camping is rather a plush experience since such amenities as hot showers, lighted bathrooms, and electric outlets are usually provided, private campgrounds abound. And if living for a few days in campers or tents doesn't sound appealing, many parks have lodges or cabins for people who want to "rough it," just not totally.

The backroads of Arkansas make a bikers' paradise. "Cycling has grown by leaps and bounds," Barton observes. "People do short-range cycling just for exercise and recreation, and a lot of people are doing touring." Both touring and mountain bikes are being pedaled through Arkansas's hills and flatlands. While people with the thin-tired touring bikes find it necessary to stay on pavement, an explorer on a mountain bike or an all-terrain bike is free to wheel down the dirt logging roads that branch off many Arkansas highways.

Hot air ballooning is a popular way to spend a clear day.

Either way, a growing number of Arkansans are taking jaunts on the two-wheelers across the state. "One thing I've heard people mention lately," Barton says, "is that there are more and more little bed-and-breakfast [inns] in these little towns up in the Ozarks, so it's real easy to plan a week-long tour. You don't have to carry a lot of luggage to do something like that." Or a lot of camping equipment, either. A change of clothes, a bit of cash, and a charge card is all that's needed, he says. "Just plan to ride wherever you have a bed-and-breakfast a day's ride away from you."

Bike racing, triathlons, five- and ten-kilometer runs, and marathons are also a growing passion of Arkansans. In fact, it's the rare town that goes an entire year without having competitors dashing along its streets in at least one of the events. The Pepsi 10-K, for instance, draws thousands each spring to race along the thoroughfares of downtown Little Rock, even crossing the Arkansas River and looping through North Little Rock for a mile or two. And what the Pepsi race is to runners, events like the annual Metric Century Ride originating at Lonoke are to bikers.

While several of the athletes who enter these are quite serious about their sports, there are many more who take part in them just for the excitement of it. "A lot of them train all year just trying to stay healthy," Barton says, "and one of those events comes along and they decide, 'What the heck.'"

Rock climbing offers adventure and scenic beauty in Arkansas's mountain ranges.

The courthouse square fills with dancers, musicians, and spectators during the music festival at Mountain View.

Tourists from all over the country take home the waters of Hot Springs.

Children join in the dancing of the Cleburne County Cloggers at the Little Rock Zoo's Zoo Days.

Yet you don't have to be an athlete in training or even someone who likes the outdoors to enjoy all Arkansas has to offer. Not by any means.

The Little Rock Zoo, founded in 1926, is the state's only zoo and one of its largest attractions. More than 350,000 people each year come to talk, walk, and have fun with the animals. Visitors from all over Arkansas and surrounding states, too, come to the Little Rock Zoo to see the lions, tigers, monkeys, and elephants.

"We consider ourselves a medium-sized zoo," says Anna Patterson, zoo education director. "We have about two hundred different species—birds, reptiles, mammals, and amphibians." That number includes about thirty endangered species, among them certain gorillas, orangutans, giant anteaters, and two-toed sloths. And very few of the animals are caged. Patterson notes that "most of the exhibit areas are moated and barless"—like the wilderness tracts built specifically for the apes and giraffes.

When the leaves begin to change into their fall colors and the air can be described as nippy, Arkansans know the state fair is not far behind. Thrilling rides. Impossible-to-win games. Sweet and gooey, fried and crispy, creamy and slippery foods. Clowns and singers and magicians. Cows, pigs, rabbits, and horses. Rodeos and rock concerts. Beauty contests and livestock competitions. The Arkansas State Fair provides it all during its ten-day October run.

"From fine country music to pig racing, there's something for everybody," John Holmes, general manager of the Arkansas State Fair, says. And that indeed is what brings close to 400,000 people through the gates of the fairgrounds in Little Rock each autumn. You can bet that as long as a child can still win a blue ribbon for a cow she raised or a beau can win a fuzzy, stuffed animal for his girl, the nostalgic, romantic spirit of the fair will live in Arkansas. No matter how modern the

Photographs on these pages were taken in the locations referenced on map.

1. *Lake Maumelle, p. 112*
2. *Mountain View, p. 117*
3. *Hot Springs, p. 117*
4. *Little Rock, pp. 118-119*

The Great Apes Display is part of the Little Rock Zoo's ever-growing collection of animals.

fair becomes—with huge topsy-turvy roller-coasters and giant "monster" trucks that smash each other up—it will continue to draw people together in the spirit of fun and adventure.

The fair, though, is in no way the only time and place Arkansans get together to have a big time. In fact, very few towns go the whole year without celebrating something, whether it's recognizing a special aspect of the area's heritage or marking its anniversary as a township. Sometimes the festivities are simply to usher in a special time of the year such as summer, the harvest, or Christmas. And any other reason to celebrate will do as well. Yet the great thing about each parade, each pageant, and each outdoor festival is that each has developed its own distinct character and traditions.

RiverFest, for example, a big Memorial Day Weekend party on the shores of the Arkansas River in Little Rock, is a festival begun by the Junior League of Little Rock that combines the best elements of a hometown picnic with a cosmopolitan spirit. Excellent planning and organization undergirds the event, which draws hundreds of thousands of people each year from around the state. Arkansas is perhaps at its best during times like these, when black, white, Asian, and Hispanic Americans, grandparents and teenagers, sit side by side on the riverbanks, rocking and clapping together to the beat as they listen to country and western, blues, or rock 'n' roll.

Vendors, flushed from the warmth of late May as well as their busy dealings with the crowd of customers, offer arts

Hundreds of thousands descend on Riverfront Park for RiverFest each year.

Kilts and bagpipes are the order of the day for the Scottish Festival at Arkansas College in Batesville. (Courtesy of Department of Parks and Tourism, photo by Craig Ogilvie.)

Forrest City's Harvest Festival is one of the many arts and crafts fairs that take place in Arkansas each fall.

The music room is one of the period rooms that can be toured at the recently renovated Marlsgate Plantation.

In Hope, watermelons are king, and the fact is celebrated each year at the Hope Watermelon Festival.

and crafts, all types of wares, and foods of every kind. Children play games in booths set up especially for them. Adults eat, shop, and take in as many of the wonderful sights, sounds, and smells of the big party as they can. And while Riverfront Park is bustling with all these people, the river is full of boats—sailboats, party barges, and motorboats anchored in the nearby waters, both witnesses to and participants in the celebration.

Later on in the summer, the Hope Watermelon Festival offers an entirely different atmosphere altogether. People flock to the southwest Arkansas town from miles around—for who can pass up a free taste of melon from Hope, the town that holds the record in growing huge, tasty watermelons? A Texas twang or a Louisiana drawl can be heard almost as often as an Arkansas accent. Seed-spitting and watermelon-eating contests are major attractions, while activities like egg tosses, arm wrestling, and cake walks produce just as much laughing and cheering. No wonder a spirit of fun and games pervades the four-day picnic.

Then, come autumn, the whole town of Helena welcomes people not only from around the state but from around the world to the King Biscuit Blues Festival. The music-filled event is the town's annual tribute to the musicians who started a whole new era of American blues—called Delta blues—from Helena radio station KFFA back in the '40s. That's when Sonny Boy Williamson and Robert (Jr.) Lockwood played the blues during the noon "King Biscuit Time" program. Now blues bands and singers come each year to deliver their own renditions of the steamy, moody music. And blues lovers by the thousands come to hear it.

The celebrating doesn't stop there. A truly party-hardy Arkansan could fill a good many of his weekends traveling around the state to any one of a wide variety of festivals—the Johnson County Peach Festival at Clarksville, Lum 'n' Abner Days in Mena, Summer Fest at Camden, Summerset at North Little Rock, International Fest in Little Rock, Oktoberfest in Hot Springs . . . and the list goes on and on.

"Take me out to the ball game" ap-

plies to more than baseball in Arkansas. You'll find Arkansans cheering and rooting at all kinds of games, from grade-school soccer to high school basketball, college football to professional baseball. Supporting a favorite team is just part of the fun of going to a game. It's also being part of the crowd. Yelling your loudest. Eating hot dogs and drinking hot chocolate. Following college team mascots in chants and silly antics, or standing and singing during the seventh-inning stretch at an Arkansas Travelers baseball game.

At certain times of the year you can watch not only people but horses or dogs race. Both Oaklawn Park in Hot Springs and Southland Greyhound Park in West Memphis offer excitement and entertainment to huge crowds. Oaklawn Park begins its season each February and runs until the final race, the Arkansas Derby, is won in April. The dog track at West Memphis, the largest in the world, races the fastest greyhounds raised. "They come from all over the country," spokesman Bill Apgar says. "We pride ourselves in having the best greyhounds in the United States running our track here." Not only do the dogs come from all over, but so do those who come to watch and wager.

Another chancy adventure, and one found only in Arkansas, is diamond hunting. Just outside of Murfreesboro

It never rains and the action never stops at the Arkansas Travelers' Ray Winder Field.

there is a huge field that looks deceptively like any other rocky field of dirt, but is actually Crater of Diamonds State Park. More than a few people have exited from the park richer than when they entered. And even those who don't can have fun searching for the tiny gems.

Recreational treasures small and large are abundant and easy to find here. Hitting a golfball or swinging a tennis racquet, swimming laps or snagging grounders, playing touch football or watching the hometown team play, climbing rocks or rocking in a sailboat—if it sounds fun, more than likely, Arkansans are doing it.

An old mine shaft stands on the grounds of Crater of Diamonds State Park near Murfreesboro, where some of the rocks you find have a special sparkle, and are yours to keep.

The Cossatot River has some of the most challenging rapids in the country.

STATE AND NATIONAL PARKS

With so much natural beauty and so many important historical locations, it's no wonder that Arkansas has forty-six state and national parks and memorials. While some are wilderness or recreation areas, others preserve interesting bits of Arkansas's past.

STATE PARKS

BEAVER LAKE STATE PARK at Rogers is a great place for nature study, since 28,000 of its acres are undeveloped.

BULL SHOALS STATE PARK at Bull Shoals, with the White River and Bull Shoals Lake, is a fisherman's dream come true.

CANEY CREEK STATE PARK, eleven miles east of Star City, has a timber-filled lake ideal for bass, bream, catfish, and crappie fishing.

CONWAY CEMETERY STATE PARK, two miles west of Bradley, is the family plot of Arkansas's first governor, James Sevier Conway.

COSSATOT STATE PARK near DeQueen contains a river that offers adventuresome floating for experienced canoeists and kayakers.

CRATER OF DIAMONDS STATE PARK at Murfreesboro is the only place in the United States where you can look for diamonds and keep the ones you find.

DAISY STATE PARK at Kirby offers camping and picnicking on the shores of Lake Greeson.

DEGRAY STATE PARK at Bismarck offers all the fun of Lake DeGray, a lodge with swimming and golf facilities, and a full-service marina.

DEVILS DEN STATE PARK at West Fork, in a valley of the Ozark Mountains, is full of caves, crevices, and rock formations to explore.

HAMPSON STATE PARK at Wilson has an exhibit of artifacts from the Mississippian Period culture, A.D. 1350 to 1700, when a people with a complex structure of civilization occupied the area.

HERMAN DAVIS STATE PARK at Manila, one acre of land surrounding a monument, honors Private Herman Davis, an Arkansan and noted World War I hero.

JACKSONPORT STATE PARK at Jacksonport takes visitors back to Gilded Age days with its restored courthouse and White River riverboat.

LAKE CATHERINE STATE PARK near Hot Springs offers water recreation and camping.

LAKE CHARLES STATE PARK at Powhatan features Lake Charles, a 700-acre lake full of bass, crappie, bream, and catfish.

LAKE CHICOT STATE PARK, eight miles north of Lake Village, is a quiet getaway in the Mississippi Delta region with fishing in the lake and camping in a large pecan grove.

LAKE DARDANELLE STATE PARK has three lakeside areas: at Russellville, Dardanelle, and Ouita. Each offers camping and access to the lake.

LAKE FORT SMITH STATE PARK at Mountainburg offers beautiful scenery and great backpacking in the Ozark Mountains.

LAKE FRIERSON STATE PARK, ten miles north of Jonesboro, is a great place to fish year-round and is popular for its dogwoods in the spring.

LAKE OUACHITA STATE PARK at Mountain Pine sits on the eastern tip of Arkansas's largest manmade lake and offers all kinds of water opportunities.

LAKE POINSETT STATE PARK near Harrisburg offers shallow-lake fishing along with camping and picnicking areas.

LOGOLY STATE PARK at McNeil, Arkansas's first environmental education state park, has eleven natural springs and unique plant life. Park interpreters give workshops on ecological and environmental topics.

LOUISIANA PURCHASE STATE PARK, located at the junction of Lee, Monroe, and Phillips Counties, marks the beginning point of the survey conducted at the time of the Louisiana Purchase. A monument and the 1815 benchmark used in the survey are preserved there.

MAMMOTH SPRING STATE PARK at Mammoth Spring is the site of the largest spring in Arkansas, from which nine million gallons of water flow every hour.

MILLWOOD STATE PARK near Ashdown offers some of the state's best fishing on marshy, tree-filled Millwood Lake.

MORO BAY STATE PARK at Jersey is a popular water sports and hunting area.

MOUNT MAGAZINE STATE PARK near Paris is a scenic area for rapelling, hiking, and backpacking.

MOUNT NEBO STATE PARK near Dardanelle, 1,400 feet above the Arkansas River Valley, offers wonderful views, great camping, and fourteen miles of marked trails for hiking.

OLD DAVIDSONVILLE STATE PARK near Pocahontas marks the site of the historic settlement of Davidson, which was established by French settlers in 1815. Fishing is popular there today.

OLD WASHINGTON STATE PARK at Washington offers a glimpse of life in territorial Arkansas with a number of restored taverns, shops, and residences. Guides are on hand to tell about them.

OZARK FOLK CENTER at Mountain View lets visitors see artisans at work and hear musicians playing Arkansas's folk music.

PETIT JEAN STATE PARK near Morrilton, rising 1,100 feet and located between the Ouachita and Ozark mountains, is a hiker's paradise with waterfalls and other interesting geological formations.

PINNACLE MOUNTAIN STATE PARK at Roland, a day-use park, offers environmental education and recreation. Exhibits are displayed in the visitors' center and the park offers workshops throughout the year.

POWHATAN COURT HOUSE at Powhatan has been restored to its late-nineteenth-century form and contains some of the oldest written records in Arkansas.

PRAIRIE GROVE BATTLEFIELD at Prairie Grove preserves the site of one of the most important Civil War battles in Arkansas.

QUEEN WILHELMINA STATE PARK, near Mena, hides in the clouds on Arkansas's second highest peak. Two inns and a lodge form the resort, which was built in the late nineteenth century by Dutch people who named it after their queen.

RED RIVER CAMPAIGN consists of three parks marking the sites of Civil War battles at Poison Spring near Camden, Mark's Mill near Fordyce, and Jenkin's Ferry thirteen miles south of Sheridan. Today outdoor exhibits, picnic sites, and hiking trails can be found there.

TOLTEC MOUNDS STATE PARK at Scott is an archaeological site under continuing investigation. The site was active in the Plum Bayou period, A.D. 700 to 950, and the people who lived there were mound-builders. Three of the mounds still stand.

VILLAGE CREEK STATE PARK near Wynne has two lakes, playgrounds, and baseball and football fields.

WHITE OAK LAKE STATE PARK at Bluff City is on a timber-filled lake and features a number of hiking trails.

WITHROW SPRINGS STATE PARK near Huntsville offers peaceful floating on the War Eagle River.

WOOLLY HOLLOW STATE PARK near Greenbrier has facilities for camping and picnicking and a small lake for boating, swimming, and fishing.

NATIONAL PARKS

ARKANSAS POST NATIONAL MONUMENT near Dumas marks the site of Arkansas's first settlement, founded by Henry de Tonti in 1686.

BUFFALO NATIONAL RIVER in north central Arkansas, with its scenic bluffs and gravel bars, is one of the most popular floating rivers in the state.

FORT SMITH NATIONAL PARK at Fort Smith marks the location of the fort established in the 1870s to keep peace between warring Indian tribes.

HOT SPRINGS NATIONAL PARK at Hot Springs is a town full of tourist attractions, but was once known best for the therapeutic value of baths taken in its naturally steaming waters.

PEA RIDGE NATIONAL MILITARY PARK at Pea Ridge commemorates the site of the Civil War battlefield.

For centuries water has gushed out of the rocks at Blanchard Springs.

Sterling Cockrill with Downtown Partnership is one of the people behind the revitalization of downtown Little Rock.

VISION

Watershed. It's a term that's often tossed around when talking about places, their histories and their futures. It refers to a time of great change, a turn toward a new direction—not a new beginning, necessarily, but a new focus. Indeed, it's a term that very well may apply to Arkansas as she prepares to enter the twenty-first century.

Our past here has not always been easy. Arkansas has suffered from being rural and poor; she's been tugged and shoved and virtually beaten down by outside forces like the Civil War and the Great Depression. And the state has suffered from her own naiveté and her stubborn refusal to recognize her best assets. She's tended to react to change instead of preparing for it and using it to her advantage.

But there are signs that that is changing, that Arkansas finally is feeling steady on her feet again after losing her balance time and time again since the initial jolt of the Civil War. A definite sense of optimism and self-confidence, qualities that characterized early Arkansas, again fills the state's legislative chambers, business board rooms, town councils, and classrooms. Arkansas has found her way back to her original course, and she's ready to join the race to tomorrow.

Bart Turner in eastern Arkansas looks over his irrigated fields, part of a farmers' co-op he established to help farmers market their crops.

Award-winning Thorncrown Chapel near Eureka Springs, designed by E. Fay Jones, offers a prime example of how innovative architecture can blend with its natural surroundings.

It's the people of this state with clear, positive vision for Arkansas's future who will lead her there. Not just economically—because if Arkansas has been a testament to anything in all her years, it's that the quality of life has little to do with wealth. But the potential for growth and happiness and, yes, prosperity, exists in all areas, from the arts to industry to medical care to ministering to the needs of the world.

Don't believe it? Read on.

Ann Chotard was ready to come home. The native Arkansan, a graduate of what is now Henderson State University, had spent the early 1960s in Colorado earning graduate degrees in the performing arts and stage direction, and had studied under some of the greatest singers and teachers in the opera world. Wouldn't it be wonderful, she thought, to bring all this back to Arkansas and develop an opera program where one had never existed? "I was naive," Chotard says of her youthful zeal. After all, the state had no foundation for the art form, no basis really to build on.

Yet, twenty years and quite a few obstacles and frustrations later, Chotard has accomplished for Arkansas more than she ever dreamed she could. Wildwood Center for the Performing Arts, an exciting development that will have an impact on the state's culture and economy when fully completed, is a result of her years of experience and work and her ability to envision what can be.

And she has plenty of experience in that respect. After developing an opera company at Henderson State University, her first accomplishment once back in Arkansas, she was anxious to perform the same feat on a state level. In 1973 the seed was planted—the seed being a $6,000 matching grant from the

*Ann Chotard looks at plans for the Wild-
wood, future home for the performing arts.*

Arkansas Arts Council. Within fifteen years, the Arkansas Opera Theatre, one of only about fifty-five opera companies in the country, had grown to a $600,000 operation.

Yet those years of growth demanded a lot of ingenuity and nurturing, especially in locating hard-to-find resources and supplies for the company's productions and educating the public about opera. "It has been an interesting challenge," Chotard says, "a kind of mission to try to bring something quite wonderful here because we do have a wonderful place to try to develop something."

Opera, like other arts, isn't only a nice supplement to Arkansas entertainment offerings. According to Chotard, much more is involved. "People take the arts—take opera, take theater—as something kind of necessary, but they are just in the forefront of understanding how important it is to the development of the state." That, she says, is where Wildwood comes in.

When an anonymous donor offered Chotard one million dollars for AOT to build and have its own theater, Chotard thought about it for a bit. Then "I asked if that vision could be expanded," she remembers. "If we could find land, we

could build a place like Wolf Trap or a Tanglewood or an Aspen." Each time Chotard visited these performing arts centers, she would find herself thinking, "Why should I have to travel to other places to see these things when we have the land and the beauty of the state?"

So Chotard found her land. Not only that, she found a number of corporate backers and a lot of support from political, business, and civic leaders. Plans for Wildwood, to be located on ninety-two acres in the western suburbs of Little Rock, include a theater with room for 700, a "village on the green" featuring a small amphitheater seating 1,000, and an outdoor amphitheater with the capacity to seat 10,000. Fundraising and construction is happening in three different phases, with the theater first opening its doors in 1990.

"It's something about thinking futuristically," Chotard says of her dream turned reality. "It's really a very farsighted view of the arts. Those things that the economic community looks at, they don't just look at the short term and say, 'What are you going to have five years from now?' They're going to look at twenty years from now." And that's exactly what she has done for the arts in this state. "Wildwood," she claims with a deserved amount of pride in her voice, "will be a national and international center, built on more of a global scale than just Little Rock. So Wildwood is a national center—it's an Arkansas center, but it has national and international implications for us."

Keeping business and industry growing in the state is another vital issue. Although Arkansas's economy was healthier in the late 1980s than at any other time in recent history, room for improvement always exists, according to Dave Harrington, who has served as executive director of the Arkansas Industrial Development Commission since 1983. And, he adds, strides toward that improvement are always being made.

"If you look at Arkansas in general, we're in pretty good shape" as we enter the 1990s, Harrington says. "We're growing in industrial jobs: industrial jobs create wealth, generate revenues, and generate other jobs." Some fields in particular—like health care and transportation—are "growing and have led in the growth and know where they're going and what they're doing and have done it well," he points out. Yet he is the first to admit that some troubling disparities also exist within the state, such as in traditional agrarian areas that are finding the transition to a more industrial economy a difficult one to make. So while "Arkansas is probably no better or no worse off than most of the states or a lot of the states in the South," steps are being sought and

Birds of prey are rehabilitated for release back into the wild.

Arkansas has many spots of natural beauty.

The skylines of Arkansas's cities are constantly changing.

made every day to ease that transition.

Harrington emphasizes that the key is for Arkansas to invest in herself, her own citizens. "We have a tremendous quality of life here that could be enhanced if we could provide better jobs for some of our people. And in order to do that, you've got to invest, both short term and long term." So new legislation and sources of increased revenues are being considered, and the AIDC is going to work—amply supplied with a number of carefully designed projects and programs—to build and improve the state's economic foundation.

The agency joins with communities, helping them develop and implement strategies for attracting businesses and industries best suited to them. It also works with existing industries to anticipate and avoid problems and maintain their vigor. Some special projects of the AIDC target small, minority-owned, and agricultural businesses that need outside support in order to grow. Other special efforts have resulted in the slate of films and motion pictures recently produced in Arkansas.

The AIDC's vision for the future, as Harrington sees it, is to combine Arkansas's best resources—hardworking people, agricultural knowledge and wealth, health- and science-related expertise—into a unified drive for a healthier state economy. "You see, we grow into the future," he said. "We ought to be nationally and internationally renowned in that particular type of growth, whether that be in agri-related, nutrition, bio-technology—whatever it might be."

Dr. Robert H. Fiser can stand in his fourth-floor office at Arkansas Children's Hospital and see for miles, past the buildings and houses of Little Rock, past the trees and green fields of the surrounding countryside, past all until blue and green meet at the horizon. But even that grand view loses its luster in comparison to the vision Fiser has for the role of Arkansas Children's Hospital in Arkansas's future. Not just tomorrow or next year, but well into the next century.

Of course, visions are nothing new for Children's Hospital. In the early 1970s, the facility decided to expand from being simply a local hospital to being a quality medical center serving the entire state. Previously, the state's wealthy took their seriously ill children to out-of-state institutions while everyone else had to settle for the care they could find in Arkansas. But Fiser and his colleagues dreamed of a day when Arkansas's poorest children would receive medical treatment on a par with that anywhere else in the world—a day when excellent care available in Little Rock would be the first choice of all Arkansans, including those who once went out of state.

The building blocks for this stronger program already existed. Children's Hospital was already an Arkansas institution over fifty years old, and the pediatrics department of the University of Arkansas Medical School was well established. When the two joined, the accomplishments of the first fifteen years were nothing less than those hoped for. "I think what we've done is to have a facility that we feel in the giving of clinical care is not only equal to (any other hospital) but that there is no place in the United States providing better care. And that's a goal I think we've achieved and will continue to try to keep."

The transition from hospital to medical center was by necessity a statewide effort. Levels of care, Fiser explains, have to be excellent at all tiers, with the pediatricians in smaller towns being trained to give top-notch preventive and primary care. Secondary care centers in larger towns around the state are able to care for children with broken bones or non-life-threatening illnesses. The role of Arkansas Children's Hospital, then, Fiser says, is "to concentrate on that tip-of-the-iceberg, hardest type of care" that requires the most specialization as well as expensive technology often not available in outlying areas of the state. "We've not tried to eliminate any competition" in the state, he adds, "but we've just tried to put all the specialists together and create a critical mass of people at Children's Hospital."

Now that that has been done, it's time to move on to the next phase of the overall plan. "Our dream of the future is

"Coping in Hope," a sculpture by Harry D. Loucks, cheers patients and their families at Arkansas Children's Hospital. (Courtesy of Arkansas Children's Hospital, photo by Tim Hursley.)

twofold," says Fiser. The goal of the first phase is to develop "a Children's Hospital without walls," one in which the hospital and its physicians can "act as a stimulus for any area of the state to help them upgrade their facilities to whatever possible." This entails stepping outside the boundaries of strict physical care for children and into a holistic approach to child development. The goal is to help a child and his family both develop to full potential in medical, educational, nutritional, and developmental aspects—hence the program's name, MEND.

MEND is envisioned as a sort of family life center. "Really, what we see," Fiser says, "is that everywhere there's a Wal-Mart, there ought to be one of these family life centers." If the program

proves to be as effective as expected, "there's going to be a tremendous need for it, particularly all over the South and Midwest." The program is already underway in places like Morrilton and Helena.

The second part of the plan, also already well in the works, is the development of a research institute at the hospital. Complementing the MEND program, research will center on improving child development. Fiser would like the scientists to be a group of "people who are almost like a basic science department who can look at the molecular genetics and the molecular biology of the brain. That is, nutrition—neuro-transmitters—how does it affect thought—how does it affect emotion?"

The impact of such study for Arkansas, he feels, could be tremendous. "We really have better clinical material in Arkansas than Harvard, Stanford, Yale, or anywhere else to answer [the question] 'What is the environment's effect on mental stages of a child's development?'" Because Arkansas is a farming state with a lot of food industries, it is a prime location for nutritional studies. For example, Fiser believes the research could easily be performed in conjunction with the chicken and rice industries here.

Another plus for developmental studies in Arkansas is having the National Center for Toxicological Research in Pine Bluff, which should facilitate research on the neurological effects of toxins. Arkansas's central lo-

Bill Worthen of the Arkansas Territorial Restoration helps to preserve Arkansas's history for generations to come.

cation and relatively stable population, which includes both rural and urban lifestyles, also stand to enhance the credibility of any prospective research.

"We're just scratching the surface" at this point, Fiser believes. "We really should be almost like a mini-National Institute of Health for children's development." He's optimistic enough about the future capabilities of Arkansas Children's Hospital that he has made a challenge to the faculty: at least one of them, he charged, should be nominated for a Nobel Prize by the turn of the century.

Yet it's the whole of what the hospital can do in the future that really excites him. If ACH succeeds in creating such a system of care, "where you follow up on all these children and find out what

Gunner Pool, northwest of Mountain View, is one of the state's beautiful natural assets.

*The view of Saddle Canyon from Route 71
in autumn shows the colors of the season.*

all goes on in their development, then our sort of dream is to take out a big ad in the *Wall Street Journal* and say we have the best facility to study children's development anywhere in the United States."

You'd think all the anticipated advances would threaten the need for pediatric medicine. "Pediatrics is the only job that would like to put itself out of business," Fiser says. "But we'll never be put out of business because there are levels of care that will really enhance quality of life." That kind of care demands the foresight and careful organization that ACH has amply demonstrated already.

Heifer Project International, Inc., another agency with a vision for a better quality of life, reaches far beyond Arkansas's borders in scope. Its original dream began during the Spanish Civil War when Dan West, an Indiana farmer, realized the futility of his job of giving food to the poor widows and orphans in Spain. The same people kept coming back day after day, no less hungry than the day before. He saw

that what was needed was a system that would help them help themselves. In 1944, West organized Heifer for Relief, a program based on the idea, "Don't just give them a cup of milk, give them a cow." David Gill, HPI education director, says that the hungry could then "take care of themselves, which is what they would really want to do." And the value of the program doesn't stop there: "Those people give the [animals'] first offspring to another needy family, so they do pay for their gift. . . . They become donors to others. The 'gift that keeps on giving' was a major principle of that early vision."

Since then, the agency's name has changed to Heifer Project International, its international headquarters have moved to Little Rock, and the original vision has expanded commensurately. In addition to providing cows, pigs, goats, and other food-producing animals to farmers around the world who are caught in the poverty cycle, HPI sends trained workers with the livestock to teach techniques of animal husbandry to the recipients. Gill says, "We've learned a lot about how to assist

One of the purposes of the Heifer Project International ranch near Perryville is to improve strains of animals continuously to help alleviate world hunger.

people in helping themselves through livestock, and we feel that with that knowledge comes an obligation to share our knowledge with others."

HPI's International Learning and Livestock Center, located forty miles west of Little Rock, plays a big role in that mission. The ranch offers a variety of educational opportunities. Three- to five-day seminars offered to men and women from various parts of the United States, Latin America, Asia, and Africa teach them practical techniques that HPI has collected from all over the world. "It's brief, it's basic, it's real practical stuff—learning how to build fences, how to give shots, how to butcher a chicken—that hands-on kind of stuff that you really need to know," Gill says.

Youth groups and organizations come the HPI ranch from around the country, giving many teens who have never lived outside the city an idea what life on the farm, especially for poorer farmers, is really like. In addition to working with the animals or in the gardens during the day, they spend time in the evening discussing Third World issues. "It enlarges their world a bit—to understand what's going on, and how our lifestyles and our values impact others, and how others impact us in this increasingly interdependent world." The ILLC staff believes that an important part of its mission is to create an awareness of world hunger issues for people who have never had to worry about a scarcity of food.

Once or twice a year Gill takes small groups overseas to work side by side with Third World farmers. "They can see these animals [given by HPI] in those villages," he said. "It gives people a chance to really see how Heifer Project does make an impact in an individual family or small village. And I've found those extremely enlightening experiences for myself and for those who've gone."

One of the most fascinating spots on the HPI ranch is the hillside farm. By combining "ideas we've gleaned from

Devil's Den State Park offers a quiet retreat for hikers and campers.

Third World countries where they've been done successfully," ranch volunteers have transformed a barren 2.5 acres of rocky soil to a farm that could support a family of five. Techniques used are efficient and ecologically safer than many of those employed by high-tech farmers in the United States. "There's a role for [Americans] in helping farmers know how to farm better, but it's a real fine line there. It's really not us teaching from American technology, it's going in and working with the local people and making it their solution, not ours." And the hillside farm, he says, "conveys our vision of what could be."

Arkansans have all it takes to foster a quality of life that's far better even than what is enjoyed today, not only for their own people but also for their brothers and sisters around the world. It begins with vision; without commitment, however, it stops there. Fortunately, Arkansas has a large number of individuals and institutions possessing both these qualities. They know there will be challenges, yet they remain optimistic, determined, and involved in the process of developing Arkansas's many resources—the pride and working spirit of her people, her natural beauty and wealth, and the potential for growth in all areas of life. Because of this, Arkansas can look ahead to the future with excitement and optimism. Chances are, she won't be disappointed.

Birds of prey circle the skies outside De-Queen.

LEADERS WITH VISION

The National Advisory Board of First Commercial Bank is proof positive that Arkansas is full of leaders with ideas and plans for the state's future. The men and women who make up this group, convened annually by First Commercial Corporation CEO and board chairman William H. Bowen, are all stories of success in their own right.

They come together in Little Rock each year to discuss, study, and make recommendations on critical issues facing the state. Some of them live here

and some have followed career paths elsewhere, but all call Arkansas home and are concerned about her future.

After each session, a report of the council's findings is published. Some of the papers produced since the organization first met in 1971 have been "The Preservation and Improvement of the Quality of Life in Arkansas," "Arkansas Tourism: The Sleeping Giant," "Energy for Arkansas: A Challenge for Survival," and "A Leadership Formula for Arkansas."

Index